CANADIAN STRATEGIC FORECAST 1994:
PREPARING TO MEET THE ENERGY CHALLENGES
OF THE 21ST CENTURY

The Canadian Institute of Strategic Studies

President, Don Macnamara, OMM, CD, MA
Executive Director, Alex Morrison, MSC, CD, MA

The Canadian Institute of Strategic Studies provides the forum and the vehicle to stimulate the research, study, analysis and discussion of the strategic implications of major national and international issues, events and trends as they affect Canada and Canadians.

The CISS is currently working independently or in conjunction with related organizations in a number of fields, including international peacekeeping; Canadian security and sovereignty; arms control and disarmament; Canada-US security cooperation; regional security studies; environmental issues; regional and global trade issues.

CISS publications include:

Free With Membership:

The Canadian Strategic Forecast
Seminar Proceedings
Strategic Datalinks
Strategic Profile Canada
The CISS Bulletin

By Subscription:

The McNaughton Papers (The Canadian Journal of Strategic Studies) (2 issues/year)

Peacekeeping and International Relations (6 issues/year)

The CISS is an independent, non-partisan, non-profit organization. For membership, seminar and publications information please contact:

**The Canadian Institute of Strategic Studies
76 St. Clair Avenue West, Suite 502
Toronto, Ontario, M4V 1N2
Tel: (416) 964-6632 Fax: (416) 964-5833**

Edited by: ALEX MORRISON
SUSAN MCNISH

Canadian Strategic Forecast 1994:

Preparing to Meet the Energy Challenges of the 21st Century

THE CANADIAN INSTITUTE OF STRATEGIC STUDIES

Canadian Cataloguing in Publication Data

The National Library of Canada has catalogued this publication as follows:
Main entry under title:
The Canadian strategic forecast
1990-
Continues: The Canadian strategic review

ISSN 0843-6940
ISBN 0-919769-74-8 (1994)
I. National Security - Periodicals. 2. Security, International - Periodicals. 3. International relations - Periodicals. 3. International relations - periodicals. 4. International economic relations - Periodicals. 5. Canada - National security - periodicals. 6. Canada - Military policy - periodicals. I. Canadian Institute of Strategic Studies.

U162.C35   355'.033   C90-039063-8

The CISS is grateful to AECL CANDU, Alberta Energy Company Ltd., The Cooperative Security Competition Program of the Department of External Affairs and International Trade Canada, Foothills Pipe Lines Ltd., and Ranger Oil Ltd. for their assistance in the staging of the seminar and the publication of these proceedings:

The Institute also wishes to recognize the following individuals for their assistance in preparing this book for publication:

- Leanne Berard
- Stephanie Blair
- Kevin O'Brien
- Dave Zeit
- Marc-Yves Bertin
- Sarah Galea
- John Zada

This volume printed and bound in Canada by Canadian Printco Limited.

CONTENTS

DOCUMENTS

Alex Morrison
Executive Director, CISS

Don Macnamara
President, CISS

Introductory Remarks

Alex Morrison

The CISS is pleased to be holding our annual autumn seminar here in Kingston on the topic "Preparing to Meet the Energy Challenges of the 21st Century."

You will notice a number of high school and university students with us today. Our student internship programme and other student activities are an integral part of the whole makeup of the CISS, and we are very grateful to those individuals and groups who contribute funds in support of them.

Our speakers today come from government, crown corporations and private industry. The subject of energy in the 21st century, we feel, is going to present at one and the same time a challenge and an opportunity to Canada as it decides how to function within a world which will become increasingly interdependent, and increasingly dependent on various forms of energy. There are tremendous events happening in the energy fields within Canada and outside of Canada which have a large number of people concerned and which will impact on the choices we have to make. We feel that the speakers we have brought here today, each of whom is willing to be subjected to intensive cross-examination on the record, will be able to present balanced views. We do think that at the end of the day we will have raised a number of questions and perhaps have answered some of the ones with which you have come here. I would now like to call upon Brigadier-General (Retd) Don Macnamara, the President of the Canadian Institute of Strategic Studies and Professor of International Business at Queen's University to say a few words and then to introduce our keynote speaker.

Don Macnamara

Good morning and welcome to our Strategic Forecast for 1994. The subject of our seminar today is "Preparing to Meet the Energy Challenges of the 21st Century." I think that it is general knowledge that energy supply is fundamental to the successful development of any economy. It is also well recognized that one does not find energy immediately on demand; it is something that has to be planned for. Therefore it is entirely appropriate as we are well into the last decade of this century that the most strategic resource for our country be examined in terms of its supply and the challenges that we will be facing in the 21st century.

Maurice Strong

Preparing to Meet the Energy Challenges of the 21st Century

Thank you for the very congenial welcome you have accorded me this morning. I am very happy to address a group assembled by the CISS, an institution for which I have a very high regard.

I appreciate the opportunity to share some of my views on the vital role of energy in strategic planning for the 21st century. The 21st century used to seem very remote and distant, but now it is less than seven years away; it has come into our short-term time horizon. I use the word "vital" when I describe energy issues because I firmly believe that energy issues are central to our future; that is obviously the reason why you have chosen this theme for your meeting today.

I am not an energy expert in the technical or academic sense, but I have been around energy issues for many years; in fact I started out my life in the conventional business world as an energy analyst. I would not qualify by today's more rigorous professional standards, but I was introduced to the energy world in that manner and I have followed energy issues for many years. Neither is this the first time that I have been in the electric power industry. When I was president of Power Corporation of Canada some years ago it was in fact an electric power organization, the largest private power holding company in Canada. I mention that only to indicate that energy has

Mr. Strong is Chairman and CEO of Ontario Hydro, North America's largest utility. He was Secretary-General of the 1992 UN Conference on Environment and Development.

been a very important part of my life for many years, and more recently I have been able to see energy issues from the broader perspective of their effect on our future, not only in terms of Canada, but indeed in terms of our future on the planet.

I am not talking solely about the dwindling supplies and increased costs of our conventional energy resources; it is well known that energy is in fact the most abundant phenomenon in our universe. As Einstein taught us, $E = MC^2$ -- energy is everywhere and everything. So there is no question of a shortage of energy, the real issues are about how we bring energy to bear on the jobs that only energy can do in our technological civilization, and about how we can accomplish this in environmentally sound and economically viable ways. These issues are not just about how to conserve and better use conventional energy resources, nor are they simply about maintaining our current standard of living. In a very real sense I am talking about the very survival of our way of life on this planet.

For those who don't know me well, I want to reassure you that I am not one of those somewhat dubious prophets who hang around street corners holding a sign reading "The end is nigh!". If I truly believed that the end was both nigh and inevitable I wouldn't waste your time and my breath talking about these issues -- I would probably be out by a lake somewhere enjoying what was left of the future of nature. I do believe, however, that humankind is at one of the most critical crossroads in its history, that we are in the midst of very fundamental civilizational change, and that that kind of fundamental change is not always easy to perceive when you are at the centre of it. I also believe that time is running out in the sense that we need to make some very fundamental changes in the ways in which we conduct ourselves, in particular the ways in which we manage and use the Earth's energy resources, and some of its other resources. The problem rests not so much in shortages of resources, but in the consequences that their wasteful, indulgent use have on the life systems of our planet.

I am not alone in this concern. Let me quote a famous statesman on the subject. He said:

> "*To waste and destroy our natural resources, to skin and exhaust the land instead of using it so as to increase its usefulness, will result in undermining for our children the very prosperity which*

we ought by right to hand down to them, amplified and developed."

That statement comes from Theodore Roosevelt at a time when environment and sustainable development were not even in our vocabulary. It was given a century ago. I believe he was talking about the need, and indeed the duty of industrialized societies, to embrace policies of what we now call sustainable economic development, many decades before the term itself was invented. The world's population in his day was about 1.5 billion; it is now more than 5 billion (5.4 the last time I looked at the meter) and in the past two decades alone the number of people on this planet has increased by an amount equal to the total in Mr. Roosevelt's time. That is an amazing phenomenon. As a matter of fact when I am asked the difference between the Stockholm Conference in 1972 and the Earth Summit in Rio in 1992, I usually reply that is 20 years and more than 1.7 billion people. In that 20 years 1.7 billion new people arrived on our planet to share a diminishing resource base, the same number approximately that existed at the beginning of our century. It is a very, very sobering thing to think about. If we look at it in other terms, the increase in our numbers last year alone was some 91 million; we are adding the equivalent of one New York City every month to the world's population.

There is overwhelming evidence that the industrialized world cannot continue in its historical patterns of production and consumption and it cannot forge ahead indefinitely on the path of profligacy in its use and its wasteful disposition of the Earth's resources, both for its own sake, and for the sake of the myriad others who have not yet experienced the luxuries of waste. The evidence for this has been mounting for some time; we saw it at the United Nations Conference on the Human Environment in Stockholm in 1972, and 15 years later the World Commission on Environment and Development, chaired by Prime Minister Gro Harlem Brundtland of Norway, provided further testimony in its landmark report *Our Common Future*. The Brundtland Commission made it clear that, since 1974, while a great deal of progress had indeed been made towards environmental improvement in isolated instances, overall the environment of the planet had deteriorated markedly, and there had been a serious acceleration of major environmental risks, such as those of climate change and ozone depletion in particular. These threats and the recommendations of the Brundtland Commission prompted the

United Nations General Assembly to convene the Conference on Environment and Development (UNCED), the Earth Summit at Rio de Janeiro, in June of 1992. Studies and preparatory work undertaken for UNCED made clear not only that the ecological consequences of our economic behaviour were worsening, but also that rich-poor disparities within and among nations were deepening and becoming more entrenched.

The recent report of the World Energy Council's Commission on Energy for Tomorrow's World supplies even more detailed evidence. Among its important findings is that energy issues will shift from the industrialized to the developing world within the next three decades, (in fact that process is already well under way), and that the latter's proportion of world-wide energy consumption will rise to some 55 percent from 33 percent in the same period. Among the many severe challenges identified is the requirement for investment of about (US)$30 trillion in the expansion of existing energy systems and technologies by the year 2000. To give you some idea of the magnitude of this, it is one-half more than the current total world GDP. Obviously, this is simply not achievable. Moreover, Energy for Tomorrow's World not only maintains that the target of stabilizing global anthropogenic CO_2 emissions at the 1990 level by the year 2020 is virtually unattainable, it says that there is a strong possibility that atmospheric CO_2 concentrations will continue to rise for many decades to come. You can't just turn it off -- it takes a long time for the processes which absorb greenhouse gases into the atmosphere to work their way through the system.

However, there is also evidence that circumstances are bringing about changes in energy consumption patterns spontaneously, without a grand strategy or concerted environment-conscious planning. In a book entitled *Vital Signs 1993* Lester Brown describes the 1990s as "the Decade of Discontinuity". It is an era, he says, in which longstanding upward growth curves for production of such key economic commodities as grain, steel and coal have suddenly reversed. World coal production, which had risen annually and almost without interruption since the beginning of the Industrial Revolution, declined in 1990, then again in 1991 and 1992. World oil output peaked even earlier, in 1979. Only the production of relatively clean-burning natural gas is expanding.

Of course that trend will not necessarily continue. It is quite clear that many of the largest countries of the world, such as China and India, are going to have to continue to use more coal unless new options emerge, which does not seem to be too likely in the near future. These reversals in historical trends, however, do indicate that many investment decisions are already shifting because of severe, albeit often localized, environmental constraints. Intolerable air pollution in such cities as Los Angeles, Mexico City and some European centres has certainly put a brake on the unrestrained growth of automobile use. When you see Los Angeles, in effect the home of the automobile culture, taking the lead in constraining the use of the automobile, it is clearly a portent for the future. It is happening elsewhere too. Recently Athens had to ban the use of automobiles in the city centre, and the same phenomenon is clearly going to have to take place in many, if not most, of the great cities of the world.

Acid rain, health concerns and the more recently acknowledged threat to the ozone layer have dramatically influenced the world's attitude towards the use of coal, even though we are not yet ready to separate ourselves fully from the fossil fuels era. A growing environmental consciousness in recent years has produced discernable improvements throughout the industrialized world in what I would call the close-in problems. If you compare life in many of the cities of the industrialized world now to what it was twenty years ago, you will find that there has been quite a noticeable improvement; the air is much cleaner and in many respects the cities are more liveable. This may not be true with regard to traffic patterns, but it is in terms of local air and water quality, and other elements of quality of life. Toxic emissions to air, land and water have indeed declined, and important changes in manufacturing processes have reduced our demands for raw material and energy. In a high-tech era, economic growth is no longer necessarily tied to increases in energy and raw materials use. This is most notable in Japan, which now uses lower quantities of raw materials and energy per unit of GDP than any other nation.

While we have taken some important first steps to come to grips with the more threatening and intractable risks such as global warming, they are only first steps, and very, very modest first steps. Indeed there is a danger that while we are making inroads against the more visible and immediate problems we could become complacent about the more remote but more broadly threatening environmental perils. Moreover, little attention has been given to the area of environment-economic relationships in the policies and practices of governments and industries. The growing awareness and concern over the past two decades with respect to the environment has been accompanied by the establishment of environmental ministries and agencies by virtually all governments. This has produced a proliferation of *ad hoc* regulation, but these activities have typically not been linked to, and have had very little effect on, national economic and industrial policies, the fundamental policies and practices of major sectors that are the principal sources of environmental impacts.

Regulation is necessary, but experience has shown that its effects can be limited and sometimes even counterproductive if it is not accompanied by changes in fiscal and economic policies that provide positive incentives for environmentally sound and sustainable development. In some ways the existence of environmental ministries, as essential as they are, has perpetuated the myth that somehow environmental difficulties and problems can be dealt with by an agency with nothing but regulatory powers. The whole theme of the Earth Summit in Rio was that, in fact, our environmental problems derive from wasteful and indulgent patterns of consumption and production behaviour in economic life and that we can only address them by making basic changes in our economic behaviour and in the system of incentives and penalties by which governments motivate that behaviour. In some sense, then, the existence of environmental ministries as an area to which governments can throw their environmental problems has to some degree been counterproductive, since very few environmental ministries have much influence on economic or industrial policies, or on the policies of agricultural and other sectors that really affect our environmental concerns.

That is certainly apparent with regard to energy, when it is recognized that, even though we deplore the overuse of fossil fuels, our whole fiscal and subsidy system is geared to promoting the most environmentally destructive of those fuels, which is coal, while at the same time penalizing with very high taxes oil and, to a lesser extent, natural gas. I realize that this has some historical basis but we are nevertheless far from relating our energy policies to the need to conserve energy and to reduce CO_2 emissions. We continue to approach the problem from the wrong end. Earlier this year a paper from Arthur D. Little's Centre for Environmental Assurance said that industry in

North America and Europe is spending more than $150 billion per year on pollution abatement and control, the "end-of-the-pipe" remedies, and that this figure will likely double by the end of the century. Despite these enormous outlays companies are still not meeting society's demands. In other words we have been busy applying very expensive Band-aids to our industrial infrastructure while natural resources and people's health and welfare, in the developing world in particular, have been haemorrhaging.

The prospect of a massive increase in Third World energy consumption over the next 30 years boldly underlines a point that I have been trying to make since well before Rio, and that is that the industrialized world must reduce its environmental impacts in order to leave space for developing countries to begin to fulfil their own development needs and aspirations. The earth simply cannot sustain another traumatic round of unfettered growth or a repeat of the unthinking exploitation that marked the first industrial revolution and which to an alarming extent continues. Inertia is a powerful force in human affairs and, even while we talk of change, the present patterns of our industrial life are deeply embedded in our culture and in our fiscal systems, and they by and large continue as before.

A vitally important first step, which makes as much sense economically as it does environmentally, is a decisive move towards energy efficiency and energy conservation. Those of us in the power utility sector have enormous potential to help our customers to cut their energy use, to make that use more efficient in economic terms and more friendly in environmental terms. With respect to both our environmental objectives and our economic objectives, there is no question that that will make us more effective and competitive. The Electric Power Research Institute in the United States, a very conservative industry-sponsored institution, has estimated that electricity use in that country could be reduced by as much as 55 percent through cost effective energy saving measures. Others think that this is a conservative estimate; that it could be as much as 75 percent, and that is without significantly disturbing our present economic patterns or our present quality of life, indeed improving both. Most electric utilities today have some sort of energy management programmes in place. I believe we are still just on the threshold of the potential savings. The irony is that these make at least as much sense in economic terms and competitive terms as they do in environmental terms. There is a similar potential in the transportation field.

A study for the National Academy of Sciences in the United States judged that straightforward technological improvements, using existing lightweight materials, for example, could make vehicles 50 percent more efficient and save about two million barrels of oil per day. That saving is more than the total amount that the US imports from the Persian Gulf region today. US President Clinton's recent initiative on lightweight cars was very encouraging; a lot less encouraging was the fate of his earlier initiative on an energy tax, the result being a very weak and inadequate tax, even though the principle was certainly in the right direction.

A second step is to reflect in our energy prices the full external cost of producing energy. As long as our energy prices remain at artificially low levels, particularly in North America, there is little incentive to develop alternatives to our current energy patterns. I am often asked about the seeming dichotomy in my position on prices, but there is a consistency, I believe, in that position. On one hand I believe that energy prices must rise, because under good market economics they should incorporate and internalize their real costs, and that includes their environmental costs; that means that energy prices must rise. The other side of it is, however, that in Ontario, (and I am speaking particularly about the rates of my own company, Ontario Hydro), we must be competitive. I think that this is entirely consistent because we cannot unilaterally increase our prices; however we can continue to use whatever influence we have to get society to move towards full cost accounting for energy which will increase the prices. But within that framework we must always be competitive. I am pleased to say that Ontario Hydro is in the process of adopting full cost accounting as a guide to our decision-making and we are pressing this within the community of public utilities. We are members of the E-7, the seven largest utilities in the world, and we are getting these issues onto its agenda. While we cannot unilaterally incorporate full environmental costs into our own rate structures until society as a whole decides to move in that direction, we hope that our example will help to accelerate that process.

A third step (and I do not mean to imply that these steps are necessarily sequential) involves a fundamental revision in the system of incentives and penalties by which governments motivate the conduct of citizens and corporations. In general terms, this means providing positive incentives for environmentally sound and sustainable energy practices, products and services, together with corresponding penalties to deter unsound and wasteful behavlour. This needs to be accompanied by full cost accounting methods at the national accounting levels as well as at the levels of individual business. It is, after all, fully consistent with the principles of market economics that the price of all products and transactions should incorporate their full real cost. That, as you know, will effect a revolution in the energy economy.

Speaking of consistency, one of the more intractable myths surrounding this whole matter of sustainable development is that energy efficiency costs more than it is worth and that conservation is somehow a recipe for slow growth or no growth. The experience of industrialized countries, notably Japan, has demonstrated that environmental improvement and efficiency in the use of energy is fully compatible with, and indeed contributes to, good economic performance. On a domestic level, Japan has been very success-ful in recent years in reducing pollution levels and energy and raw materials consumption per unit of GDP, while continuing, until the recession, to lead the world in economic performance. In the process, it has created a whole new generation of competitive advantage for Japanese industry. Keidanren, the primary Japanese industrial association, and MITI both issued state-ments which indicate very clearly that they believe that the new generation of industrial opportunity is going to be environment-driven, and they are demonstrating that. Their energy costs are much higher than ours and that has driven their move towards a more effective use of energy.

The principal sources of added value and competitive advantage in the new global economy are capital and knowledge of applied technology, through marketing, through management and design, etc. Those who have only their labour to sell will increasingly require specialized training and skills. It will be, and in fact is now, a much more selective and demanding labour market and one which, frankly, is going to continue to affect many of our people. Thus we have the paradox in which the measures we take to make our economy more efficient and our companies more competitive may succeed in creat-ing a bigger pie, by creating a more efficient economy, while at the same time diminishing the size of the pieces of that pie available to the less privileged sectors of society who are disenfranchised by this process. I am convinced that addressing the increasing dichotomy between the haves and the have-nots will be the principal challenge to industrial societies, as well as to relations between industrialized and developing nations in the period ahead. It is an issue for which there are no easy answers and we have barely begun the process of grappling with it. When I see what we are doing in Ontario Hydro, in the human sense it is agonizing, even traumatic; we have had to lose 10,700 people in ten months. It is almost a third of our total work force. It had to be done in economic terms and in competitiveness terms, but think of that in human terms, multiply it all across society. Every day we see, on television and in the financial pages, more evidence of so-called downsizing. Yet there have been no real policies to date to address the questions that arise as to how the people who are being left out of this process are going to find a productive place in our society.

All of this is deeply relevant to Canada, and the energy industry is at the very heart of the interface between the environment and the economy. Virtually every environmental issue, from a local dumpsite to the deterioration of the global climate, has an energy dimension. This gives us a special responsibility to lead the process of transition to a sustainable energy economy, and for Canadians that responsibility is heightened by the fact that we are the most energy indulgent nation in the world, even allowing for the vastness of our territory and our cold climate. At the same time Canada is faced with the need to effect a massive restructuring of its domestic economy to ensure that it can continue to compete in an increasingly competitive and interdependent global economy. The present recession is not just a traditional recession; it is in fact the product and the evidence of a fundamental transformation in our economic life. Most of our companies and our customers are caught up in a dramatic process of downsizing through severe cost cutting measures and staff reductions. These have responded not only to the most prolonged recession since the Great Depression of the 1930s but also, as I have said, to some basic structural changes taking place in our economies. Ontario Hydro is in the final stages of a restructuring and cost reduction programme that has reduced our ten-year capital expenditures budget by some $24 billion, our operating, maintenance and administration costs by an average of over $1 billion a year, and reduced our regular staff by 6,700 and 4,000 full-time contract employees. This is a rather radical change responding to the needs of our customers and the need to bring the spiralling increase in our rates to a halt. The only way to do it is to cut costs. We have reorganized the corporation along the lines of business units in order to make it more competitive and customer oriented in every phase of our operations. We are at the same time reshaping the organization to live up to the corporate goal, recently adopted by our Board of Directors, which is to help Ontario become the most energy efficient and competitive economy in the world and a leading example of sustainable development. Ambitious, certainly. Some may even say pretentious. But we deliberately wanted to set a high standard for our own performance and perhaps even to throw down a gauntlet to other utilities in other jurisdictions because there is no way in which we can maintain the good life we have had in Ontario, and the sound economy we have had in the almost half-century since the end of the Second World War, unless we have a basic commitment to more efficient use of energy.

The Business Council on Sustainable Development, which comprised some 60 CEOs of the world's leading corporations -- people who are not wild-eyed environmentalists, but rather some of the world's leading industrialists -- made it clear that the pathway that we face in the future cannot simply replicate what we have done in the past. Efficiency is the key to competitiveness and it is the key to environmental sustainability. The two things come together. We in Hydro have just received the report of an internal task force on sustainable development, chaired by two eminent environmental leaders, Jim MacNeill and David Runnalls. The report contained a series of recommendations which respond to the Global Agenda 21 adopted by governments at last year's Earth Summit in Rio. We are determined to make Ontario Hydro, as a major factor in the Ontario economy, a much more active and positive force for revitalizing the economy and helping to make it more competitive. Energy efficiency is our highest priority. Our first challenge is to set an example to others. In this we have a long way to go. Our sustainable development task force pointed out that we are our own best and worst customer -- best because we use in our system 50 percent more electricity than the entire city of Toronto -- just within our own organization. We are the worst customer, however, because we don't pay for it; it is treated as a free good in our own internal economy. We intend to change that, to charge our own business units on the same basis that we would charge our customers. This way we hope to get more energy efficiency and better business decisions. What we are doing at the micro level at Ontario Hydro is something that needs to be done throughout the world.

I don't think most Ontarians realize what a big dinosaur Ontario Hydro really is. Based on last year's figures (we haven't done a calculation since our recent reductions) its budget is higher than the national budgets of more than 75 percent of the nations of the world, with all of the paraphernalia, presidents, prime ministers, cabinets and civil services, etc. that go into national budgets. That gives you some idea of what it is like to turn around a giant of that kind, but we are determined to do it, and I think we are well on the way. The stakes are high. We estimate that we can save 800 megawatts inside Ontario Hydro just by using energy more efficiently within the corporation. That would be almost like discovering another Niagara Falls; and not only do we not have to build a generating station to get that power, we hope to produce an additional savings or additional revenues of some half a billion dollars per year. That is just by being more efficient ourselves. Most organizations could find, to varying degrees, similar savings. Ontario Hydro has been working with its own customers in this regard, including some very large customers, to help them to use our product more efficiently.

Unless we succeed at becoming more energy efficient our economy will not be more competitive and our customers will not continue to be customers; they will not make investment decisions to bring more jobs to Ontario or even to maintain the jobs that are here. This is true not only of Ontario but around the world. We cannot have a competitive economy in Ontario unless our energy economy is competitive, and that energy economy, to a very considerable extent, depends on our rates. We have to keep those rates stable and competitive. What better example could the power industry set for the nation as a whole than for each utility to commit itself to the same kind of process of self-examination and the development of its own "Agenda 21" that we have just been doing while at the same time encouraging and working with its customers to improve their energy efficiency? While this may seem counterproductive to utilities like Ontario Hydro, which have substantial surpluses of capacity and declining revenue, as I have said, it makes sound economic sense.

I have just come back from China where we have initiated a new Asia Power Group in cooperation with our neighbours, Hydro Quebec and Power Corporation of Canada. Some would say "what are you doing off in China -- you should be looking after the homefront." Well the homefront is our priority, but we have been in the international business for a long time. We now have capacities and expertise and experience that is marketable, that can help us reduce the pressures on our own customers while at the same time making an important contribution to the development of economies like those of China, which are really on a growth path. Just to give you one example, the Chinese told me that if they could be just as energy efficient as the world average, which is pretty poor, they could save 350 million tonnes of coal per year. To put it another way, if China were to become as energy efficient as India, which is certainly not very energy efficient, China could double its GNP without adding at all to its greenhouse gas emissions. It is in our interests to help them do that, it helps to create markets for our services and our expertise, but at the same time, it is in our fundamental interest to help them to make their energy economy more efficient.

I realize that none of this will be easy, nor does it even seem timely to some when the pressures of recession and competition are most acute. It is not easy to manage this process when our own revenues are moving down for the third year in a row, but I believe that these changes are imperative in both economic and environmental terms and that this period of transformation is precisely the right time to effect these changes; after all it is at a time of disruption and crisis when you can often move most expeditiously in implementing fundamental long-term change. Waiting until what may seem to be a more propitious moment would, in my view, exact heavy costs both in terms of our economies and in terms of the viability of our own organizations.

I know that these issues have been on your mind and I am delighted that they are on your agenda. Energy has had a long and important security, as well as an economic and political, dimension. If you take a look even at such things as the recent Gulf War you will see that energy deficiency, the dependence of North America, in particular the US, on external supplies of oil, is a driving factor in terms of international strategic and security policies. It will continue to be as fundamentalism spreads in the areas of concentration of oil and gas resources in the Middle East, and nuclear energy faces a crisis of confidence that it has not yet overcome. Yet our appetite for energy has not diminished. Even energy efficiency has limitations. We can immensely improve our environmental and economic performance through energy efficiency which is why, on a world basis, we must concentrate on energy efficiency; but that is not the ultimate answer. It buys us perhaps 20 years if we do it really effectively, but it is not going to eliminate the need to find permanently more acceptable forms of meeting our energy supplies. Price is very key here. Prices need to be higher, as I have mentioned; we need to reflect the full cost of energy and those higher prices will also drive energy efficiency and conservation.

Environmental security, in my view, poses a more important challenge to the world community than any security risk in our history. We face together, in the danger to the very life support systems that make productive life on this planet possible, a greater risk to our ultimate security than we have ever faced from each other. We have not taken that in yet. But there is a lesson in this and that is that when we are convinced that our security is at risk we have always been willing to respond and do whatever was necessary. This time environmental security comes cheaply, frankly, compared to conventional security. Conventional security requires us to put billions and billions of dollars into things that, if not used, simply have no other economic use; even if they are used, then they are doubly destructive. In contrast, environmental security can buy us a new round of economic regeneration and job creation, and the use of the opportunity base that the technological civilization has opened up to us. So I believe that in the achievement of environmental security we can at the same time achieve a new era of economic revitalization and enfranchisement, and I do not see any place in the world that is better positioned than Ontario to do it. Ontario Hydro cannot do it alone of course, but as the largest single organization in this province and one of the largest utilities anywhere, I believe we have an important responsibility to take the lead and that is what we have been trying to do.

Forum

Ian Wilson, Canadian Nuclear Association

I have a few questions that relate to your comments regarding Japan. The Canadian Energy Research Institute has published studies which indicate that much of our apparent energy profligacy in Canada is due to our highly-intensive energy resources and the production in resource-based industries which result in Canadian exports. This distorts the picture in comparisons between our energy consumption per unit of GDP and the consumption of Japan.

Second, Japan seems to have developed a strategy of moving towards less energy intensiveness in its economy by increasing its electricity-intensiveness with the deployment specifically of non-fossil fuelled supply options such as nuclear. They have placed ten orders this year for new nuclear units.

Third, could you discuss how we can overcome the tendency to juxtapose the demand for efficiency options against the supply options as though they were mutually exclusive as opposed to being complementary, as indeed they should be?

Mr. Strong

You are correct, of course, that there are some justifications for Canada's energy intensiveness. They may provide a certain offset but they do not negate the basic assumption that we have a tremendous amount yet to do in improving our energy efficiency. Look at what has happened in some of the major resource industries. INCO, for example, has moved from being an inefficient energy operation to the single most energy-efficient mining and smelting operation of its kind in the world. So we have shown we can do it in individual instances but the very thought that some of our major corporations are finding that they can be a lot more energy efficient, that it makes good business sense for them to do so, underlines the point I was trying to make -- that we have a long, long way to go.

In terms of Japan, there is no question that the Japanese have really relied more and more on nuclear power for electricity generation. They continue to rely on nuclear and their public so far has accepted this whereas the publics in other countries have not done so to the same extent. Also, in strategic and security terms, the Japanese are very aware of their vulnerability when their supplies of oil are threatened; they were frightened during the crises in the Middle East, for example, and this has driven a great deal their reliance on nuclear.

There is no doubt that nuclear is not going to go away -- in Ontario Hydro, for example, half our base load is nuclear and nuclear is a fact of life. What is in doubt at this stage is the degree to which nuclear will be a primary source in the future. That depends on a lot of things, with public acceptance and confidence being very important, but also cost. If Ontario did not have an official moratorium on the development of new nuclear projects, we would in any event have an effective economic moratorium at the moment, and I cannot predict what the future of nuclear will be here. There may well be a renewed nuclear future, but it will not simply be an extension of past experience, with huge megaplants concentrating the risks in particular areas and therefore, in a sense, magnifying them. These make very large targets for anti-nuclear public opinion, and when they go wrong, when they do go off-track cost-wise, they can impose very major and very permanent costs. For instance Darlington was a technical triumph, but it was a financial disaster. It started out costing $3.5 billion and ended up costing $14.5 billion, and that is incorporated into our debt structure and it is one of the reasons for our rate increases; it is not the only reason, but it is an important one. So I would say that the future of nuclear is still up for determination. As I see it now, there probably is a future for nuclear. Certainly there is in Japan. For Canada, however, I think it is a more open question.

You point out that energy efficiency versus looking at the supply options is not an either-or situation. Of course it is not. As I tried to imply in my statement, energy efficiency is not an ultimate answer. We need to build it into our system and what it can do is give us some time to examine our supply options more fully. At Ontario Hydro we are taking a whole new look at long-term supply options. We have a surplus right now, but that surplus will not last forever and we cannot take it for granted. So you are quite right, we do have to examine our long-term supply options in relation to energy efficiency and energy conservation. They are indeed complementary and mutually supporting and in many cases, energy efficiency is the best economic alternative in the short term.

Julian Donald, Kingston Collegiate and Vocational Institute

You mentioned that Ontario Hydro has a budget that would rank among the top 25 percent of the national budgets of the world. But how does Ontario Hydro rate in relation to other large corporations, in particular large multinationals?

Second, in terms of nuclear power and hydroelectric power and their environmental impact, how do they relate in comparison to each other and to other energy sources?

Mr. Strong

On the first question I can't provide the exact figures, but Ontario Hydro is either the largest or the second largest corporation in Canada, depending on what criteria you use. If you use assets or income, we are certainly not the most profitable at the moment. Internationally we rank as either the third or fourth largest utility in the world, and utilities are very big companies. We are bigger than any utility in the United States including TVA or Pacific Gas and Electric. I do not say that with pride, particularly, because bigness isn't necessarily a virtue; in fact it has some accompanying difficulties, but we are large by any international standard. We are certainly no General Motors, but we are of one of the larger corporations in the world.

As to the environmental effects of nuclear and other energy sources -- there is no single source of energy, apart from energy efficiency, that is environmentally benign. Fossil fuels create greenhouse gases, CO_2 emissions, which are a threat, as we know, to the climate control system that makes life possible on our planet. That is a very unique system. Why isn't there life elsewhere? Why wasn't there a human type of life on this planet for most of its existence? Because that delicate heat balance is something that is very rare and unique and we are now changing it; we are changing the filter and when we do that we are going to have some effects that we may not be able to predict exactly.

So, CO_2 emissions from fossil fuels create a major problem, and nuclear does not create CO_2 emissions. Two major nuclear issues are still not adequately resolved. First is the public's fear of the consequences, however small they might be, of a nuclear accident. Those consequences are exacerbated by the size of nuclear plants and by the badly managed, badly designed, badly maintained plants in Eastern Europe which pose a much greater risk than plants anywhere else. We have a very good record in Canada with our CANDUs but nevertheless there is a risk that the public perceives. The other thing is waste disposal. That is still an unresolved issue and while it has been quiescent, people have not been attentive to it, it has been a problem.

So it is a balancing act. None of these sources is devoid of environmental impacts and it is hard to make an actual trade-off. If you think that climate change is the biggest issue, then of course you go nuclear or at least you put more weight on nuclear, and there is a strong case for that. But let me make a final point on nuclear. At the moment it is economics that is primarily deterring major new nuclear initiatives. So there is no absolute answer, and again that is why energy efficiency is so important because we not only defer the need for major new supplies -- we don't obviate it but we do defer it, giving us some more time to examine the alternatives -- but at the same time we reduce the environmental impacts by reducing our energy use.

Michael Evenson, Royal Military College, Kingston

You refer to a rather optimistic report in the United States concerning the energy efficiency of vehicles. The NRC in the United States earlier this year published a report which made far less optimistic predictions for energy efficiency and this was partly because the cost of gasoline in the United States was not predicted to go above $1.50 by the year 2005. If that is the case, the argument was that the customer would not be prepared to pay more for his vehicle than he is likely to save over the period of time that vehicle was serviceable; in other words, it is just not worth buying a car that is more energy efficient. I wonder if you have any comments on that and on the price of gasoline in the United States.

Mr. Strong

First of all I did not predict the degree of effectiveness that might accompany President Clinton's initiative. I applauded the intent of the initiative but I would certainly agree that the ultimate result will depend on economics. Customers will make economic decisions, that is why I laid so much emphasis in my remarks on the need for governments to revamp the system of incentives and penalties, to build real incentives into that system to do the more sustainable thing. You cannot expect people as customers to do things that go against their economic interest; some may, but you cannot depend on that. So I do agree that the results of this initiative are uncertain and will depend on the initiatives and particularly on the gasoline price.

I cannot predict the gasoline price. I think it is going higher over time but not necessarily a lot higher in the next two or three years. There could be moments in which it skyrockets again because major disruptions from the Middle East could occur at any point in time, but barring that I think it is really a question of what governments do by way of taxes. I think estimates indicate that the price of oil could go up to approximately $30 a barrel without any significant economic disruption due to consumer resistance. After that you start to get some of both. The question remains as to whether that premium of $12 or so over present prices will go to governments through a tax or will be preempted by the producers, but I think such an increase is inevitable over the next decade.

Rick Fisher, National Defence College, Kingston

You have repeatedly emphasized the need for rates to be competitive, and that Ontario Hydro cannot act alone. You have cited what should be done and some of the dangers which may lie ahead, but I am interested what your realistic prognosis is and, with whatever degree of specificity you can offer, what you are expecting action-wise of which of your competitors. What do you think they are likely to do in response to what, for instance, Ontario Hydro has done?

Mr. Strong

We have to remember that competition is not just a question of what alternative fuel or energy supply might be available to one of our present customers, but also what alternatives that customer has available for moving jobs, for moving new capacity outside of the province. It is that kind of competition that is really most dangerous to our economy. Industrialists are making decisions on whether or not to expand their plants here; for example, will Goodyear realize its potential to quadruple its production at Napanee? It can, but a lot will depend on energy prices. The same is true right across the board. So it is not just the direct competition from an alternative source of energy here, it is the competition we face from alternatives that our customers have. I think they are just doing the same as we are with regard to trying to get their prices down. I believe, however, that we can compete, we have started the process. I think we have cut our costs more than any utility has done in an equivalent period of time. But 75 percent of our costs in Ontario Hydro are fixed, largely by our debt, and we have to have equity in our system, we have to reduce that debt, we have to move away from 100 percent debt financing, but we have to make our costs competitive.

We have done quite a lot in that direction, but there is more to do. We also need a more flexible rate structure. The Power Corporations Act under which we operate does impose real rigidities on our ability to make rates that will help save jobs and help attract new industry. We need that flexibility. So we are not there yet, but I think that we are on the way.

Brent Lewis, Royal Military College

I agree with you, Mr. Strong, with regard to the surplus of capacity that Ontario Hydro now has. However, as has been pointed out by my colleague Mr. Ian Wilson in a speech to the Municipal Electric Association in their session in the early 1980s, Ontario Hydro had an overall reserve capacity of 47 percent in 1982 with 9,200 megawatts of capacity still under construction in Pickering, Bruce-B, Darlington and Nanticoke. However, over the next seven years as oil consumption dropped, that surplus was needed to counter a five percent per year growth in electricity, which was double Ontario Hydro's predictions. In 1993, as a result of the present recession, we again have an overall reserve capacity of 46 percent, but in this case we have zero capacity under construction. It is important to note that if we assume a 25 percent reserve capacity as needed for normal operations by Ontario Hydro's figures, and if Ontario were to experience the same rate of growth as in the 1980s, the province could only sustain four years of low growth before needing new supply. This latter fact assumes that Bruce-A will not be retired for rehabilitation and retubing and that, indeed, bringing on a new generating station takes 14 years. What are your long range plans?

Mr. Strong

Regarding surplus, it is not true that we have nothing, that we have suddenly abandoned the supply side of our business. We have a large, large surplus; we have just made an arrangement to integrate over time our system with that of our neighbour, Hydro Quebec, something we have not really done before. We have a lot of non-utility generation (NUGs) anxious to get on line and we are anxious to encourage them. Frankly we have not been able to, as this community knows well, and we are not going to for any more than we have to for another couple of years. But we do look at non-utility generation as an important source.

We are very mindful of our supply options, but we do not want to repeat the mistakes that have been made in the past. We do not want to build megaprojects which result in major over-capacity that may load our rates for many years to come. I believe that the next round of supply options has to be much more diversified, that we should be willing to accept generation by others, including NUGs, and we should do it competitively. In other words, we should be inviting competitive bids for a new supply and I think we will move to that.

That is basically my own philosophy. I am in the difficult position of having to act monopolistically during this interregnum period to secure our financial integrity -- to ensure the integrity of the corporation because Ontarians have a tremendous investment in that -- while believing that we must take the lead in moving into a much more competitive, open market place.

Gail Tyerman

International Influences on Canadian Energy Policy

It is a great pleasure and honour to be here with you today. I am looking forward to a productive exchange of views.

I have been asked to discuss energy policy formation in Canada. My colleague from the Department of Natural Resources will outline in a more comprehensive fashion than I can some of the considerations involved in the development of Canadian policy. However, nowhere is it more clear than in the energy sector that Canadian policy makers do not develop policy in a domestic vacuum.

The globalization of both energy and capital markets precludes any government from ignoring the international political and economic environment. One has only to mention the price of oil and its determining impact on energy project decisions to recognize the influence of global factors on domestic energy decisions. And no single country, not even Saudi Arabia, can alone set the price of oil.

The energy industry itself also reflects a growing globalization. Key oil producing states such as Kuwait, Venezuela and Russia are opening their energy sectors to foreign investment. Canadian companies are a part of this trend and can be found increasingly abroad. Not only are they selling energy and energy related products and services but also they are engaging in

Ms. Tyerman is Deputy Director of the Energy and Nuclear Affairs Division, Department of External Affairs and International Trade Canada.

energy exploration around the world. Hence, industry looks to governments to create stable trading and investment conditions where such activity can flourish.

While Canadian firms can be found in all parts of the world, clearly the American market, currently taking about 80 percent of our energy exports, will continue to be crucial to Canada. The Free Trade Agreement plays an important role in setting the conditions for trade in energy with the United States.

I will provide you with some background on the evolution of energy policy approaches of Western governments generally, and the international context in which Canadian policy is made.

As both an importer and exporter of energy and energy intensive products, Canada has helped shape the evolution of international policy approaches and in turn has been influenced by international developments. In my view, the international energy agenda will continue to play an important role in our energy policy formation for the foreseeable future.

The 1970s and early 1980s saw in all Western countries intense government interest in the energy sector. This was motivated primarily by the oil shocks of 1973/74 and 1979/80 and was driven by considerations of energy security. The creation of the International Energy Agency (IEA) at the end of 1974 was itself a consequence of those concerns. The IEA International Energy Programme commits members to act cooperatively in any oil emergency and, over the long term, to reduce dependence on oil. Western government policy was often *dirigiste,* involving in many countries the setting of detailed targets for the energy sector, subsidies, and other financial incentives including support for major projects, price controls, government-to-government deals for the purchase of oil, and other barriers to trade. These interventionist policies reflected both the perception of the energy situation as governments saw them and the general climate of active government involvement in the economy.

Since the mid-1980s, there has been a significant reduction in detailed government intervention reflecting:

- the easier world energy and oil situation,

- a general change in government attitudes towards economic policy, and,

- unhappy experience with some government interventions.

Governments have come to recognize that energy policies should be applied in a manner so as to enhance economic growth and to support the efficient functioning of healthy and transparent energy markets. Price controls have been lifted, subsidies reduced and barriers to trade in energy removed. In some countries, state-owned energy industries have been transferred to the private sector. This reduction in government involvement is continuing. However, in no Western country has it reached a point at which the government treats energy just like any other commodity. Some special controls remain. All governments recognize that energy is not the classical example of a market commodity and there are legitimate areas for governments to set the framework conditions to govern the proper functioning of the energy markets. An obvious example is the need to ensure that decisions on future energy mix balance the concerns about environment and economic development. The IEA has made some explicit cross-cutting recommendations to its member governments. These relate to making energy markets work, to unleashing competitive forces, to encouraging trade, to removing fuel subsidies, to getting prices right and to improving the transparency of costs. These recommendations are challenging member governments, including Canada.

Last June, the 23 IEA members agreed at the ministerial level on shared goals for the development of their energy sectors to contribute to sustainable economic development and on a policy framework to achieve these goals. The major elements of this framework are:

- longer term energy security requires diversity, efficiency and flexibility of energy supply, including the use of nuclear and hydro power;

- energy systems should be able to respond flexibly and promptly to energy emergencies;

- sustainable development requires that decision-makers minimize the adverse environmental impacts of energy activities just as environmental decisions should take account of the energy consequences;

- increasing energy efficiency both of power generation and of energy use needs to be encouraged;
- research, development and deployment of new energy technologies should complement energy policy and be undertaken with cooperation from the private sector and non-member IEA countries;
- undistorted prices are essential for efficient markets; prices should include environmental costs based on the principle of polluter pays;
- free and open trade and a secure framework for investment contributes to efficient energy markets and energy security.

In the future, there will be increasing energy demand from a much broader range of consumers. According to the most recent IEA energy outlook, developing countries are expected to lead the growth in energy demand by a more than 120 percent increase by the year 2010 due to growth in population and income. This compares to an anticipated 30 percent increase in Western countries and stable demand in the countries of the former Soviet Union (FSU) and Eastern Europe. Large scale private sector participation will clearly be required if adequate investment and technology are to be applied to meet global demands.

Demand for oil and coal is expected to continue to grow, but natural gas will become an increasingly more important energy source. Such an increase in use of natural gas responds to its significant supply potential and on its perceived environmental superiority over other carbon-based fuels. Use of renewable energy will increase faster than other sources but, given its relatively small contribution today, it will still not be a significant source of energy over the next 20 years. This could have consequent negative implications for efforts to limit CO_2 emissions.

Russia, and other countries of the former Soviet Union, particulary Kazakhstan, have the potential to become important suppliers of oil and gas. The former Soviet Union controls 40 percent of the world's proven reserves of natural gas. Oil production in the former Soviet Union peaked in 1988 and could continue to drop throughout this decade. Some even predict that Russia could become a net importer of oil in this decade. However, most observers believe this situation is due more to aging technology, equipment shortages, and reservoir management practices than to a lack of oil reserves.

Russia and its neighbours are now engaged in a social adjustment of un-precedented scope. The daily lives of several hundred million people are being fundamentally re-oriented. Transition from a command to a market economy cannot be accomplished overnight, and we all recognize this. The key to success will be the maintenance of momentum. However measured, transition must not be put into a long holding pattern, or frozen, if economic activity is to be encouraged. Nowhere does this principle have more direct application than to the petroleum industries, since these industries themselves hold the clearest prospects for immediate and viable returns -- not just for investors, but for the governments and citizens of those states, who stand to benefit directly from the economic multiplier effects of increased and more efficient activities by those industries.

In the Department of External Affairs my principal duty has been the negotiation of the Energy Charter Treaty. Its focus is precisely this area of oil and gas production in Russia. Under negotiation for two years now, the Charter is intended to create a legal and market framework to attract foreign investors to Eastern Europe and the countries of the FSU in the energy sector. Western investors are clearly interested in the oil and gas sector in Russia and other FSU countries. I understand there are already about 50 joint ventures currently producing oil in the FSU, with 31 in Russia itself, including five Canadian companies. But significant capital investment will require a transparent and certain investment regime as well as secure access to markets, primarily in Western Europe.

Canada is interested in the Charter for both economic and political reasons. We wish to anchor Russia and other Eastern European and FSU countries inside a market-oriented, prosperous, and democratic system. We see the Charter exercise as one means of encouraging the necessary market and government economic reforms. We also see the logic of facilitating a diversified supply of energy for future global energy demands. At the same time, we wish to ensure that Canadian investors and sellers of energy-related goods and services can operate on a level playing field with their Western counterparts.

In the development of global supplies of energy, governments clearly have a central role in establishing the ground rules. Many would argue that this also holds true for the demand side of the equation. There are many policy tools available that, for example, governments can use to promote specific increases in energy efficiency and to encourage changes that would not likely take place under free market conditions until much later. One can think of energy taxes, mandatory efficiency standards, effective public information programmes, and incentives for relevant research.

Issues of real concern to Canadians, such as global warming, are by definition beyond the scope of national control. It is clear that the environmental challenge of increased energy use, particularly increasing carbon emissions, will need to be approached by a mix of measures and fair burden sharing among nations.

In developing Canadian energy policy, we will need to reflect this emerging international consensus on environmental concerns. More specifically, we will wish to ensure that options put to decision-makers take account of our international commitments, including the provisions of the most recent conventions on bio-diversity and climate change approved in Rio last year.

I want to mention Canada's nuclear energy policy as an example of the interaction of international and domestic pressures as well as the balancing of political, economic and technical concerns. Canada has had significant nuclear exports since the Second World War. We are the world's largest producer of uranium, producing 30 percent of world demand in 1992. Furthermore, Canada has also exported nuclear technology: there are four of Canada's unique CANDU nuclear reactors abroad and two more are currently under construction.

While there had always been a policy of exporting nuclear material for only peaceful purposes, the 1974 Indian "peaceful nuclear explosion" based in part on technology contributed by a Canadian-made CIRUS research reactor caused Canada to reinforce its nuclear cooperation and export policies. Canada now engages in nuclear cooperation only with countries that sign a bilateral Nuclear Cooperation Agreement, comprising strict Canadian conditions. These include being a signatory to the Nuclear Non-Proliferation Treaty or equivalent, full-scope safeguards, and acceptance of controls on re-export of Canadian technology and equipment, reprocessing and high enrichment. Canada currently has 16 such agreements. It is one of the duties of my division to evaluate the political and commercial considerations involved in concluding such agreements and then undertaking the negotiation of the agreements where warranted.

Since 1974, many states have complained that Canada's nuclear non-proliferation policy caused our nuclear exports requirements to be too strict; as a result, Canadian companies have missed commercial opportunities. At the same time, there are legitimate public concerns about the possible proliferation of nuclear weapons. While some activists are opposed to any nuclear power in principle, others are prepared to tolerate exports as long as strict controls on their use can be enforced. Canada has worked with other major nuclear suppliers to develop stronger agreed rules for all nuclear exports.

Nuclear power is perhaps one of the most striking examples of the need for governments to balance competing demands in the energy field. If you were to invite me next year to a similar conference as this one, I might choose to illustrate this point with the example of the need to balance the demands of energy and environment.

I hope today that I have given you a taste of some of the international aspects of energy policy formation in Canada. All governments face the challenge of promoting sustainable development not just inside their own borders but on a global basis. I hope that exchanges such as this conference will increase our understanding of the issues involved as we look toward the future.

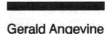

Gerald Angevine

The Importance of Energy in the 21st Century

I have been asked to speak about the outlook for energy supplies, and what the world and Canadian energy supply outlook may imply for Canadian energy policy in the 21st century.

There is potential for a significant increase in the utilization of renewable energy resources, such as solar, wind, biomass and hydro power. However, my remarks today are focused on the outlook for the primary non-renewable energy resources: natural gas, coal, uranium and crude oil.

Coal

At the end of 1992 the world had proven recoverable coal reserves amounting to about one billion tonnes. Proven reserves are that portion of potential supply which has not only been discovered but measured, delineated or estimated with some degree of confidence. The term "recoverable" indicates that it is feasible to produce those reserves under today's economic conditions.

Unlike crude oil and natural gas, world coal reserves are fairly well distributed -- 24 percent in North America, 20 percent in Asia, and 30 percent in Eastern Europe and the former Soviet Union. Australia has nine percent.

Dr. Angevine is President of the Canadian Energy Research Institute.

The remaining 17 percent are located in Western Europe, the Middle East, and Latin America.

Together, Asia and Australia accounted for 38.5 percent of world coal production in 1992, (China alone accounted for 25 percent). North America accounted for 26.5 percent, and Eastern Europe and the former Soviet Union about 20 percent. The remaining 15 percent was produced in Western Europe, Africa, Latin America, and the Middle East. While rich in oil and gas, the Middle East has very little coal.

Generally speaking, coal is consumed in the world region where it is produced. North America is the main exporter and Western Europe the main importer. The Asia-Australia region has been experiencing the most rapid growth of coal production and consumption.

Last year's world coal production of 4.5 billion tonnes was equivalent to only 0.4 percent of proven recoverable reserves. To put it another way, at last year's consumption rate the world would have enough coal reserves to last 232 years. And because actual coal reserves are much greater than proven reserves, the world has enough coal to meet foreseen needs for many centuries to come.

What is Canada's situation with respect to coal? Canada's proven recoverable reserves of coal are in the order of 6,600 mega-tonnes. Most of this is located in western Canada.

Canadian coal production last year was about 66 mega-tonnes. Not all coal is used as an energy source. A substantial portion of the bituminous coal produced in Canada is metallurgical coal which is used as coking coal in steel-making. Thermal coal production is projected to increase because of export opportunities. This does not mean that there will be a shortage in the supply of Canadian coal available to meet Canada's energy requirements. The Canadian coal reserve and production data which I have used suggest a reserve life index of 100 years. This compares with the estimate of 140 years calculated by British Petroleum PLC which used a somewhat higher reserve estimate. Both estimates suggest that Canada may be worse off than the world as a whole when it comes to coal. This, however, does not tell the whole story.

Potential additions to Canada's proven recoverable coal reserves are substantial. This is indicated by the fact that the volume of discovered coal resources "of immediate interest" is about 12 times greater than our proven recoverable reserves. It therefore appears that this country has sufficient coal to meet Canada's requirements for several centuries to come.

Uranium

The world's supply of uranium is also fairly well distributed. Twenty-eight percent of the uranium classified by the Uranium Institute as being reasonably assured at a cost of less than (US) $80 per kilogram lies in Africa (half in South Africa) and 25 percent is located in Eastern Europe and the former Soviet Union. Australia has 22 percent of world uranium resources in this classification and North America, 18 percent. The remainder lies in Asia, Europe and Latin America.

World uranium production was 35.5 million tons in 1992. At 9.4 million tons, Canada was the largest producer, followed closely by the Commonwealth of Independent States (CIS). Together, Canada and the CIS accounted for slightly more than half of world production. The rest was mainly produced by Niger, Australia, France, the US, South Africa, Namibia, and the Czech and Slovak Republics.

At 1992 production rates, and with the indicated reasonably assured supplies, the world has enough uranium to last 60 years and Canada, enough to meet the current annual demand for Canadian uranium for 29 years. This does not mean that Canada will run out of uranium in 29 years. Canada has significant uranium resources which have not been included in the Uranium Institute's reasonably assured resources classification. Moreover, if the price of uranium were high enough, it would be cost effective to reprocess and recycle spent uranium fuel.

Because of the potential for reprocessing, and because there are substantial additional uranium resources, the uranium resource life indices indicated for Canada and the world are very conservative. There is unlikely to be a shortage of uranium in the next century and the availability of uranium to use in nuclear power plants is not likely to be of concern.

Natural Gas

Unlike coal and uranium, world reserves of natural gas are not evenly distributed. Together, Eastern Europe, the CIS and the Middle East hold more than 70 percent of the world's proven recoverable reserves of natural gas. In comparison, the industrialized countries of Western Europe, North America and Japan have less than 10 percent of world gas reserves. Ultimately, this means that natural gas supplies will have to be piped or shipped rather long distances from source to consuming region.

World natural gas production totalled 72.1 Tcf (trillion cubic feet) last year or 1.5 percent of world reserves. At that annual rate of production there is enough natural gas to meet world needs for 65 years. If one were to include potential gas reserves, the reserves-to-production ratio would be more than double that. It is very unlikely, therefore, that a shortage of natural gas will develop during the next century even with increased demand because of population and economic growth and environmental policies which favour the use of gas.

Canada's proven recoverable reserves of gas, at 96 Tcf, represent about two percent of the world supply. This volume includes 25 Tcf of undeveloped "frontier" reserves, including 14.4 Tcf in the Arctic Islands and 10.6 Tcf in the MacKenzie Delta-Beaufort Sea area. The 96 Tcf also include 24 Tcf of gas reserves in western Canada's producing regions which are not yet connected. Our total natural gas resources, including proven and potential reserves, are in excess of 650 Tcf.

Last year Canada produced 4.2 Tcf of gas and consumed 2.1 Tcf. The difference of 2.1 Tcf represents net gas exports. These have risen substantially since deregulation of the natural gas industry in 1985.

The relatively large volume of gas exports to the US should not be of concern given Canada's extensive reserve base and the economic benefits which Canada derives from gas development, production and transportation. Because of the economies of scale which our gas exports allow, the cost of gas production from northern and frontier supplies will almost certainly be less in an open market environment.

At the 1992 production level, Canada's proven recoverable reserves of natural gas would last 24 years. However, when frontier gas and unconnected reserves are excluded from the total, the reserve life ratio is only about 11 years. This compares with an R/P (reserve/production) ratio of 9.4 years in the US and of 27.6 years in Western Europe. For the world as a whole, the reserve life index is 65 years as I have indicated. Given the extent of Canada's natural gas resource we will have more than enough gas to meet domestic and export demand through the next century.

As I have mentioned, the same situation applies worldwide. However, because gas reserves are concentrated in the CIS and the Middle East, security of gas supply will be a matter of growing concern in Japan and other countries which do not have enough indigenous supplies to meet their own requirements.

Crude Oil

At the end of 1992 the world's proven recoverable reserves of crude oil stood at 1,007 billion barrels. An enormous 66 percent of that amount lies in the Middle East. 12 percent is in Latin America, mainly in Venezuela. Eastern Europe, the CIS and Africa combined also account for 12 percent. North America, Western Europe, Japan, Asia, and Australia hold only 10 percent of the world's crude oil reserves.

The lop-sided distribution of world oil reserves had a lot to do with the rise of OPEC and affects the cartel's market power today. The United States' need to meet about half of its crude oil requirements by imports was a major determining factor in the US involvement in the Gulf War.

In 1992 the distribution of world oil production was somewhat more evenly divided than that of crude oil reserves. The United States, with only three percent of world oil reserves, produced almost as much oil as Saudi Arabia. Total Middle East production was only 28 percent of total production, compared with the Middle East's dominant share of world oil reserves. Latin American countries produced 13 percent, Canada and the US combined, 16 percent, and the former Soviet Union, 14 percent.

Canada's remaining established reserves of crude oil, including bitumen, were estimated by the National Energy Board at 7.9 billion barrels in 1991. This compares with the 7.6 billion barrels reported in British Petroleum's 1993 Statistical Review.

If other discovered resources and estimated recoverable oil resources not yet discovered are included, it is thought that Canada has about 343 billion barrels of oil which could be produced. To put this into perspective, Saudi Arabia's proven recoverable reserves are estimated at 260 billion barrels.

Most of Canada's oil resource, 307 billion barrels, is bitumen lying in the Alberta oil sands. The difficulty lies in the cost of producing it -- especially the huge capital expenditures which are required up front.

A more recent look at Canada's oil reserves is provided by the Canadian Association of Petroleum Producers (CAPP). The Association estimates that at year end 1992 Canada had remaining established reserves of 5,908 million barrels of conventional crude oil. In addition, we had developed non-conventional supplies totalling 2,971 million barrels. Nearly 60 percent of the conventional reserves and most of the developed non-conventional reserves are in Alberta.

Canada produced 633 million barrels of conventional light and heavy crude oil, synthetic crude oil, bitumen, and pentanes plus in 1992. Given Canada's proven recoverable reserves of conventional crude oil and equivalent, and developed reserves of non-conventional crude oil sources (synthetic crude and bitumen) that rate of production could be maintained for only about 14 years. If we look only at our conventional reserves and production the reserves life index is 11.8 years according to CAPP figures. This is somewhat higher than the R/P ratio of 9.6 years estimated by BP which, in turn, compares with 9.8 for the US and 43.1 for the world as a whole.

It is very unlikely that a shortfall in global oil supply will develop in the 21st century. With the R/P ratio as high as 43 years for proven recoverable reserves, with substantial undiscovered reserves yet to be found, and with improving technology in relation to oil exploration and production it is virtually certain that there will be sufficient oil to meet demand through the next 100 years. At some point, however, the real price of oil is likely to begin to increase as more remote reserves, which are more costly to get to market, come into play. When this happens it will slow the growth of demand and encourage development of non-conventional oil reserves such as the Alberta oil sands.

Security of Oil Supply

Comparing the reserve life or R/P ratios for Canada and for the world, Canada is in the weakest relative position with regard to oil. We are assured of secure long-term supplies of coal, uranium and natural gas. However, if our oil sands resources are not developed further, Canada is almost certain to become a net importer of crude oil by the early part of the next century, probably between the years 2000 and 2010.

Is the prospect of dependency on other countries for oil cause for alarm? Given the supply of crude oil that will be available on a global basis for many years to come, the main concern is what would happen if Canada's flow of crude oil from overseas were interrupted as the result of hostile actions taken by other countries or for any other reason. For some, the possibility of interruption would be justification enough for some sort of preventative or protective action. For others, the cost of prevention exceeds the benefits; they would advise us simply to take our chances.

The actions which Canada could take to improve the security of its oil supplies may be grouped into demand-side and supply-side categories.

Among the demand-side measures, the provincial and federal governments might do more to reduce the quantity of oil consumed by encouraging more efficient use of oil and greater use of alternative transportation fuels, especially compressed natural gas. President Clinton's drive to secure a very marked improvement in the efficiency of gasoline consumption is a welcome initiative.

Other demand-side actions that could be considered include an oil import fee or tax designed to make oil more costly and slow the growth of consumption of refined petroleum products. The downside of this is that it would be inflationary and would affect a wide range of manufacturing costs. An import fee would make it difficult for Canadian companies competing in the US and other foreign markets.

Canadian federal and provincial governments could increase gasoline taxes. Because the average tax on gasoline is much lower here than in Europe this might be acceptable to the politicians.

The authorities could also facilitate the substitution of heating oil by other fuels and encourage the use of non-renewable energy sources where this would displace oil.

Among supply-side measures that could be considered are incentives for frontier exploration and development, and measures to increase bitumen production from the oil sands, including greater support for research into more efficient oil recovery technologies and for pilot/demonstration projects.

The authorities might also consider putting a strategic petroleum reserve in place to provide crude oil supplies in the event that the flow of crude oil from overseas is interrupted. The US experience in developing a strategic reserve is illustrative. In the current situation, with Atlantic Canada and Quebec virtually totally dependent on imported crude oil but with the country as a whole still a net exporter of oil, the reserve required to meet our import requirements for, say, a three-month period, would not be very large. However, as Canadian oil production declines and the country becomes more heavily dependent on imports the reserve required will increase.

Conclusion

Canada is well endowed with each of the four non-renewable energy resources which I have discussed. In this respect, Canada is in an enviable position among the industrialized countries. However, we are but one generation away from having virtually depleted our producible conventional crude oil reserves. For this reason we must use our remaining oil reserves, and all of our energy resources, prudently.

I have identified measures which could help prevent Canada from becoming as dependent on foreign crude oil as we otherwise might become. Perhaps by the time Canada's production of conventional crude oil has fallen to the point where we could become very heavily dependent on foreign crudes, and a net oil importer, the price of oil will have risen and technology will have advanced sufficiently to make rapid development of our oil sands resources feasible. But this may not turn out to be the case and we may become and remain net oil importers for many years.

On the world scene, population and economic growth will increase demand for energy commodities during the next century. Energy demand growth and structural shifts in the market shares of the non-renewable energy commodities will be only partially offset by government environmental policy initiatives.

Economic development in Latin America, Asia and elsewhere, and the more efficient use of energy in today's industrialized world, will alter the share of energy consumption in the industrialized and developing communities. The developing countries are together becoming the world's major energy consumer. This will become more and more evident as we get into the next century. An important consequence of this shift in the geographical composition of energy demand will be that today's industrialized countries will have to compete for energy supplies more and more, and with greater intensity, with the developing countries. Barring technological breakthroughs involving new and lower cost energy sources, this suggests that the prices of energy commodities will gradually be bid up.

Robert Lyman

Perspectives on the Current Realities Confronting Canadian Energy Policy

I am pleased to be here to participate in this seminar, and I would like to thank and congratulate the organizers of this event for pulling together a program which is both provocative and timely.

I have been asked to offer some perspectives on the current realities confronting Canadian energy policy. I would like to begin by taking some time to outline the importance of the energy sector and to review some of the factors influencing it.

The impact of energy on the Canadian society and economy is pervasive. Consider the following facts:

- The energy sector absorbed 17 percent of total investment in the Canadian economy in 1992. Energy exports accounted for 11 percent of Canadian exports and the sector contributed nearly seven percent of our GDP;

- Canada is one of the most energy-intensive industrialized countries in the world. Energy consumption per household is higher in Canada than in almost all other countries;

- Energy production is a mainstay of Canada's regional economies. In the Western provinces, it makes up 14 percent of GDP;

Mr. Lyman is Senior Director, Energy Policy Branch, Energy, Mines and Resources Canada.

- Access to competitively priced, secure energy is critical to the competitiveness of many of our major export industries, such as petrochemicals, pulp and paper, and smelting and refining;
- The energy sector presents Canadians with important environmental challenges. For example, production, processing, transportation, and consumption of fossil fuels account for over 90 percent of all greenhouse gas emissions.

In short, energy touches all aspects of the lives of Canadians, as consumers and producers. As a result, government policies focusing on this sector have been and will continue to be a matter of concern to all Canadians.

I would like to take a few minutes to review what I see as the broad evolution of Canadian energy policy since the discovery of the Leduc oil field in Alberta in the mid-1940s. Since that time, Canadian energy policy can be divided into three distinct periods. What distinguishes these periods is not the policy objectives pursued, but rather the means by which they were pursued.

The first period began in the late 1940s and was characterized by the growth and development of the energy industries. The policy focus in this period was on developing the energy sector, promoting security of supply, and ensuring that the economic benefits of energy development accrued to Canadians. Throughout this era, through the early 1970s, the government took an increasingly active role in the economy at large and in the energy sector in particular. Its role was one of a promoter and supporter of energy development, as an integral part of Canada's industrial expansion. The events of the 1970s changed perceptions of the role of government in the energy sector. When the first major oil crisis hit in 1973-1974, governments throughout much of the Western world intervened to deal with what they perceived as an economic threat posed by price volatility and insecurity of oil supplies.

This marked a second period in Canadian energy policy. The approach initially followed could be characterized as crisis management. Most OECD governments, including Canada, used the policy levers available to them to implement emergency plans, protect and promote domestic supplies, stimulate energy conservation and, in some cases, control prices directly. In Canada, policy in the 1970s and early 1980s tried to insulate the country from the impact of world oil markets. Energy strategies emphasized the drive for energy self-reliance, the need for Canadian ownership and control of our energy resources, price stability, and appropriate revenue sharing amongst governments and industry.

By the early 1980s, energy policy began to change again. In part, this was a reflection of the fact that our economy is closely integrated with the rest of the world. Policy actions were based on a conviction that Canadian energy markets, to operate efficiently, need to reflect and move with world markets. This market orientation, which marked a third policy phase, resulted in a reduced role for government in the energy sector.

Today, most Western governments base their policies for energy security on the flexibility and diversity of our energy systems and the capacity of markets -- except perhaps in the case of emergencies -- to balance supply and demand effectively. At the same time, however, a growing appreciation of the environmental impacts of energy production and use led to demands for continuing government involvement.

In summary, since the Second World War, Canada has experienced an era of booming energy development in which producers were the major force; a crisis period when consumer interests were dominant; and, more recently, a period in which markets have been relied upon to establish the balance between consumer and producer interests.

During these periods Canadian energy policy objectives were expressed in different ways. They have, however, focused generally on two principal themes: (1) assuring Canadians secure, reliable access to competitively priced energy supplies; and (2) ensuring that the development of Canadian energy resources and technologies for producing and using energy affords maximum economic benefit to Canada.

Since the mid-1980s, and especially since 1988, a third dominant theme has emerged: that of environmental responsibility. I will speak more about this theme later.

So much for the past. What about the future?

Over the coming months, the new government will be taking stock of the trends in Canada's energy sector and determining how best to support its future economic health and its contribution to the well-being of Canadians. This examination will be influenced by various economic and institutional forces currently buffeting the energy industries and all levels of government. Fiscal restraints, for example, will limit government ability to participate financially in private energy ventures. This makes it particularly important for governments to work with industry and to take into account the impact of possible policy measures on investor confidence.

Since the mid-1980s, successive segments of the energy sector have undergone major, and often very difficult, restructuring. There is every reason to believe that this trend will continue and expand. The financial health of energy companies will depend heavily on their ability to respond quickly to rapidly evolving market conditions and to attract the investment needed to continue this adjustment.

A particularly important economic trend facing energy policy is the integration of energy markets and its impact on the various energy industries. The increasing integration of energy markets makes it difficult for Canada, or individual provinces, to insulate themselves from external energy sector developments. Similarly, all jurisdictions find that they are less able to develop and implement energy policy unilaterally. Autarchy, at least in the energy domain, is very much a thing of the past.

Energy prices, determined primarily by international market conditions, will continue to be a key determinant of how the energy sector operates. In the short-term, international oil prices may be volatile, due to the continuing problems of OPEC in maintaining discipline among its members over production levels and developments in the former Soviet Union. However, many forecasters now project relatively stable market conditions over the remainder of this decade. This implies that oil prices will remain roughly flat in real terms over the next three to five years, possibly with more downside than upside risk.

The increasing integration of the North American natural gas market is having a major impact on the development of Canada's natural gas industry. Deregulation in both Canada and the United States is allowing supplies of natural gas to move with increasing freedom, provided transportation capacity is available. The evolving market conditions in the natural gas markets are reflected by the price. Over much of the latter part of the 1980s, excess supplies of natural gas depressed its price and discouraged drilling activity in Western Canada. The recent improved balance between demand and supply for natural gas is expected to result in prices rising modestly, but continuously, over the immediate future. These rising prices are supporting the sector's recovery. The renewed strength of the natural gas industry has also resulted in large part from its successful restructuring over the past few years. Reduced operating costs have put the industry in a good position to exploit new markets.

In contrast to the natural gas industry, the oil refinery industry continues to face strong market pressures to adjust. The Canadian refinery industry is currently experiencing excess capacity, depressed product prices, and low profitability in response to lower demand for refined products. Several refineries have closed as the industry has sought to restructure itself in the face of these market pressures. Restructuring is essential if the industry is to regain economic health, but further refinery closings may prompt concerns about the impact on security of supply and on local economies.

Adjustment pressures brought on by increasing market integration and evolving domestic markets will be particularly strong in the electrical utilities over the coming years. Many utilities are concerned about the financial risks facing them in undertaking large new capital investments. As well, they are trying to resist financial pressures to push up utility rates faster than the general price level. In response to these concerns, many utilities have trimmed back their capital spending plans.

The economic recession, coupled with slower growth in electricity demand and excess generating capacity, has had an important impact on the domestic nuclear industry. The adjustments undertaken by the electrical utilities have placed domestic sales of CANDU reactors on hold, perhaps until the end of the century or beyond. In contrast, the international outlook for CANDU and its related technology and service is quite positive.

A complex set of pressures for energy policy stems from concern about the environment. However, further significant challenges lie ahead. Climate change, for example, has become a matter of global concern, with potentially far-reaching implications for fuel choice, energy use and lifestyle. Canada is now committed to the goal of stabilizing carbon dioxide emissions at 1990 levels by the year 2000. The new government will wish to consider what additional targets to set.

The inclination of governments at all levels in Canada to date has been to address greenhouse gas emissions reduction through an approach in which the public and industry are asked to take first those measures that make sense in economic as well as environmental terms. Even within this ambit, however, there are at least three major questions to be answered.

First, which measures should be taken because they are economic from society's perspective; that is, because they offer benefits to society as a whole that exceed their costs?

Second, assuming that private individuals will be motivated by self-interest to take those measures that are economic in private terms, what measures should be taken to "bridge the gap" between those things that are economic from private and social perspectives? In other words, what blend of taxes, subsidies, regulations, and public sector investments should be used to attain environmental goals?

Third, where major public expenditures will be required to reduce greenhouse gas emissions, who will pay for these? Which level of government, which group of taxpayers or consumers will bear the direct or indirect costs?

There continues to be a great deal of discussion surrounding these questions. For public policy advisors, the challenge is to present the choices as clearly as possible and to ensure that, for any specific set of measures, there are reasonable tools available for assessing their likely impact and for monitoring progress. For the Canadian political system, however, finding solutions to the climate change problem will test to the limits the ability of our institutions to forge consensus.

It is not only with respect to the environment that global trends have a major impact on energy policy formulation. Globalization has changed the role that governments play in the energy sector, as well as the range of policy instruments available.

We live in an era where international commitments increasingly determine the scope and manner of government action. In the International Energy Agency, for example, we cooperate to ensure that our collective oil security is enhanced, but we also adhere to several common principles that we have agreed should guide the formulation of energy policy. Elsewhere, trade agreements set out many legally binding commitments as to how we will deal with energy trade and investment issues. Energy decisions are also affected by environmental commitments we have made in various international conventions and protocols.

Within Canada, federal, provincial and territorial governments must cooperate. As owners of the resources within their borders and as the owners of many electrical utilities, the provincial governments are extremely important decision-makers. Without their cooperation few, if any, federal energy policies can be translated into truly "national" policies.

In conclusion, today's energy policy makers have less room for independent action than in the past. Globalization and international commitments limit the scope for unilateral national action. Constitutional realities and financial pressures impede large scale financial participation in the energy economy by the federal government. A strong desire by all stakeholders to be involved in decision making underlines the importance of a consultative approach to policy making. It also requires that policies be tested before a broader audience, and that consensus and partnership be forged far more than in the past.

Can we succeed in such circumstances? In the past, conflicts over national energy goals have sometimes caused bitter disputes and worsened interregional tensions. The competition among policy goals, particularly those relating to the economy and the environment, calls for tradeoffs no less difficult than those we have faced in the past. Do our political institutions have the maturity to forge collaboration and compromise today? They will surely be put to the test.

Forum

Mr. C.R. Nixon

Ms. Tyerman, in your talk you mentioned the Rio conventions. I have read very carefully the biodiversity and the climate change conventions, the forestry statement, Agenda 21 and the Rio Declaration. While they may be the best that the United Nations can do, I am left with a feeling that they are hedging, that there Is not a lot of substance to them. What do you see coming forward in the way of an international ability to achieve the CO_2 reductions which Mr. Lyman mentioned?

Mr. Lyman, you mentioned that, along with many other countries, Canada has undertaken to limit these emissions to 1990 levels by the year 2000. We are now four years into the 1990s and we have only six years left. As far as I can tell from the published data, Canada's emissions have in fact continued to increase every year since 1990. You, as an operating public servant, and I as a former one, both know that even a government with the best will in the world cannot get out a policy within two years. Also, have we, or any developed nation, ever done anything to improve the environment which caused a reduction or a setback in the standard of living? We have had a reduction in the size of automobiles, and an improvement in their efficiency, but these positive measures seem to have been counteracted by an increase in the number of automobiles on the road together with larger mileages being travelled. Could you comment on that?

This session was chaired by Mr. C.R. Nixon, former Deputy Minister of National Defence, Member of the Canadian Association of the Club of Rome.

Finally, Dr. Angevine, for the three years that you talked about, what is the absolute value of total primary energy consumption and production in the developed and developing regions of the world?

Ms. Tyerman

Very briefly I would like to say one or two words about the value of international instruments in general, and then more specifically about reaching the CO_2 emissions targets that were agreed to.

I spent four years at the United Nations in New York negotiating a lot of these kinds of agreements, many of which used to have the sort of loopholes you are referring to. I think when you have a large number of countries coming together these are the natural result, but in fact these agreements *are* worth more than the paper they are written on. The process itself can be worth more than the product in the sense that we are developing international consensus. I do not think, for example, that we would be talking about the environmental aspects of energy if this forum were held ten years ago, yet there were people and pressure groups negotiating those kinds of resolutions internationally then, moving us towards this point. As to the actual text of the conventions, you are probably right, but that is as far as governments were prepared to go at the time.

With respect to reaching the targets, I am certainly not an expert on that, but as I was preparing for this seminar I read quite a lot of the International Energy Agency material and certainly it is concerned that we are not on schedule to meet those targets by the year 2000. The IEA discusses a number of scenarios, such as increasing energy taxes and so on, that might be used, for Western countries at least, in order to advance progress in this respect. I think it is clear at the moment that the international community is not reaching those targets, but to a certain extent the targets are valuable in that they at least give us something to aim for. It gives the international community and citizens such as yourself somewhere to hold governments accountable and to use that as a pressure tactic.

Mr. Lyman

First, on the issue of whether we will be able to attain the targets either at the global level or in Canada, frankly, I don't think anyone knows yet. I think it is fair to say that within Canada the measures that have been put in place to date at the federal, provincial and other levels of government, and those measures that have been taken voluntarily, which are extremely important, will, on the basis of the best current forecast, not succeed in attaining a stabilization goal by the year 2000. What that says is that there is probably a need for additional measures, and governments at both federal and provincial levels have been consulting on that quite extensively over the course of the past several months. In fact we will be meeting again this month to try to define what the package of measures will be. It is apparent from statements made during the election in October that the new Liberal government intends to make that issue a priority.

Your question as to whether the government has ever taken an action that will hurt in order to attain environmental objectives is posed in an interesting way. I think that those involved in private industry, either as producers or major consumers of energy, could provide a long list of measures that have been imposed in order to try to reduce the adverse environmental consequences of economic activity in Canada. That is to the good; by and large most responsible firms acknowledge that it is part of good corporate citizenship to try to reduce those impacts. The level of investment that is required, for example, in the Canadian oil refining industry to reduce emissions levels is enormous. There are also higher levels of investment in the electric utility industry to reduce emissions of sulphur dioxide and nitrous oxide. These higher costs mean that there is less money available to spend on other things that we all want as a society. In a sense that is hurting, but I think it is a trade-off that most Canadians accept.

Dr. Angevine

The share numbers that I used in my final set of statistics were drawn from the 1992 publication by the IEA, entitled *Global Energy: The Changing Outlook.* The absolute numbers that the you asked about are given in detail there. For 2005 one would have to do some calculations. Based on that material, my estimate for the year 2005 total world primary energy consumption will be 11,400 million tonnes of energy equivalent and of that the 57 percent that will be coming from the non-OECD countries will be 6,498 million tonnes of energy equivalent. That leaves 4,902 from the OECD countries. That compares with the situation in 1989, which was quite a bit different as I indicated;

of the 7,815 MTOE total in 1989, 3,987 came from the industrialized countries that are members of the OECD.

Mr. Donald Lawson, Atomic Energy of Canada Ltd.

Dr. Angevine, you indicated that there may only be a 60-year supply of uranium, and that could be interpreted as limiting the prospects for nuclear energy. I would like first to make some comments and then ask you whether you agree. The uranium industry is really doing no prospecting at present. There is a surplus in supply; in fact we in Canada have been very fortunate in that we have extremely rich resources in Saskatchewan. In the past uranium could be mined if the ores were about one percent grade; now we have an average 10 percent grade in Saskatchewan, and that virtually eliminates anyone else looking for uranium at all. Uranium is not easy to find. The uranium mines in Saskatchewan were not obvious from the surface and they take a lot of exploration. With no exploration going on it is not surprising that there are very few predicted reserves right now. Uranium is fairly plentiful; it is in Saskatchewan in vast quantities; and in sea water, in low quantities.

The point of my comment really is that, if we are led to believe that uranium is in short supply, we will start to make technological changes accordingly; but today's thermal reactors use only about one percent of the available energy from uranium. If uranium is in short supply, then we would have to move to fast reactors which use about 60 percent of the available energy but are more expensive and a more difficult technology.

In my view it would be far more economic and productive to look for more uranium than it would be to look for changes in the technology. Furthermore, for a nuclear reactor the cost element of the fuel is about three percent if you take in the uranium itself, so we could afford a fast increase in the cost of uranium before we would significantly influence the cost of nuclear electricity. Also, there is another source of energy that could be used, particularly in a CANDU reactor, and that is thorium; there is almost as much -- if not more -- thorium as there is uranium. And since we are talking about energy in the 21st century, there is no doubt that some time in that century, fusion will come along and deuterium is very plentiful. I think this puts a different perspective on the indication of a limit of just 60 years for nuclear fuel. Do you agree?

Dr. Angevine

Yes, I agree with your remarks of an economic nature; I cannot pretend to speak for the technical aspects. What I referred to in conjuring up the resource-life index for uranium were the reasonably-assured resource statistics from the Uranium Institute. As you know they have another category of estimated additional resources which in itself is substantial, and if we combine the two we would see, as I indicated, that the resource life of uranium is indeed much greater than 60 years. We have such an abundant supply of economically-available uranium on the surface of this planet either proven, so to speak, or thought to be there that I don't think one needs to take a different approach to the technology.

Col. Martin, National Defence College

My question concerns ownership of the energy industry. Canadian ownership was an issue in the past, but given that the Crown essentially owns the resources, and given the regulatory tools available to the provincial and federal governments to control the use of the resource, do you see ownership as an issue for the future?

Mr. Lyman

That is very much a policy question and let me answer the way any public servant would have to answer just after a new government takes office. The recent trends in Canadian ownership of the petroleum industry have indicated a slight drop, and more recently a modest increase in levels so that we are still at the stage where about 60 percent of the Canadian petroleum industry is owned and controlled in Canada. The previous government's position was that it was not necessary as a matter of public policy to restrict access of foreign capital to the industry in order to ensure that the government would be in a position to influence the industry on those matters of public concern. Consequently, they essentially eliminated the Canadian ownership and control requirements that had previously been in place. I don't know what the attitude of the new government will be on these questions. I think that they will probably want to, at a minimum, observe the extent to which the current pattern of ownership and control in the industry is leading to levels of investment generally, and perhaps to research and development in particular, and to other aspects of corporate citizenship. That would really require much stronger intervention on the part of the state.

Mr. Bob Weaver, National Defence College

Dr. Angevine, you mentioned supply-side measures such as import taxes and diversifying sources. I was wondering how that fits in with the Free Trade Agreement, NAFTA, and perhaps GATT. Are we going to have that kind of flexibility in the future?

Dr. Angevine

Certainly there are many things that the Canadian government and the provincial governments can do to encourage greater conservation and efficiency. So long as we are not seen to be unfairly subsidizing Canadian industries that compete with other countries, I do not think that we would get into difficulty.

There are other things that we might do to attract foreign capital. For example, we could develop our bitumen resource, and I would expect, given the size of US demand and their requirements for oil, that a good deal of it could eventually flow south. So I don't think that the Americans would be upset if there were indeed some government incentives or backstopping to facilitate more rapid development.

Mr. Jan Rainey, Student, KCVI

I am very worried about our society's heavy dependence on fossil fuels. It seems that these are creating a great environmental hazard, and I am not sure what kind of world I am going to live in later in my life. Does the Canadian Energy Research Institute have a role in the promotion of research and development into alternative sources of energy such as solar energy, as opposed to simply examining current energy sources? If that is the case, could you please elaborate on what the Institute is doing to examine these alternatives, and if not, could you please talk from your perspective about the importance of these sources?

Dr. Angevine

That is an interesting comment. The Canadian Energy Research Institute is a non-profit organization funded by industry and governments. The governments are represented by the energy departments of British Columbia, Alberta, Saskatchewan, Ontario, Canada, and the Northwest Territories for the most part; we do get some support from other government organizations such as the California Energy Commission. On the industry side, there are about 130 companies that provide us with support on an annual basis. That includes most of the major and medium-sized oil and gas producers along with a good many of the smaller ones, and some coal producers. We also have involvement from pipeline companies, from the financial community, a number of the mining companies and major industry energy consumers. What we do is determined by those organizations and their representatives on our Board of Directors.

We have done a lot of work on oil and gas supply. We have done some work on the renewables and on alternative energy and I expect that we will be doing more of that in the future. At present we have a study under way on the economics of the electric vehicle and implications for energy consumption and the environment. We have a study that we are just beginning, comparing the economics of off-grid technologies for electric power generation, looking at solar, wind and bio-mass sources of energy. So we will be looking at solar and wind in that context.

We have also looked at alternative transportation fuels, alternatives to gasoline and diesel such as compressed natural gas and ethanol. So our focus is not limited only to oil or gas, or on the energy supply-side of things. One other study we are doing that is of interest, given the major portion of energy consumption that comes from the transportation sector, is one on transportation-demand management. It looks at what measures municipal governments can take to alter patterns of transportation. We have also done some work in the demand-side management area more generally, for example, looking at measures utilities and energy boards can take to ensure that the utilities themselves are doing what they can to avoid unnecessary growth in energy consumption. In fact, conservation demand-side measures may themselves be regarded as an alternative source of supply.

Mr. David Taylor, Student, Frontenac Secondary School

My question is along the same lines as the last one: it has to do with renewable sources of energy. Right now we are heavily dependent, probably almost totally dependent, on a few finite resources for our energy. In 60 years, perhaps, we are looking at running very low on these resources. We could therefore become very dependent on countries in OPEC for our energy resources. It is a rather frightening prospect to be completely dependent on a small number of countries for what is essentially our livelihood.

Mr. Lyman, what policies are in place or are being considered to deal with the inevitable changeover from complete reliance on non-renewable energy sources to renewable, sustainable ones, and what incentives are being offered to encourage energy research and development in this area?

Mr. Lyman

Let me try to answer your question factually and then offer a comment. Within the government of Canada we have a program of research and development on energy sources which covers virtually the gamut of opportunities on both the supply and demand sides.

Over the course of the past decade we have spent many millions of dollars on photovoltaics, wind energy, various passive and active solar applications and other opportunities, not to mention the most significant renewable energy in use in Canada today which is hydroelectric power. In fact, by comparison with most other countries in the world, we have a very substantial portion of our electrical energy provided by that significant renewable energy resource. The further development and use of renewable energy is not necessarily primarily dependent on the level of research and development that we do in this country. We are very much a part of the international community in that regard. I just returned from spending a week in Germany as a member of an IEA review team looking at German energy policy. The Germans are spending the equivalent of 800 million Deutschmarks over the next five years on research and development into energy, and a substantial portion of that budget is in photovoltaics and wind energy; they have a continuing subsidy for wind energy production which is provided by their rate structure in electric utilities.

Developments in the OECD region are fairly promising. They do offer opportunities for technological breakthroughs that will lower the cost of renewable energies to the point where they may become a significantly larger part of our total energy mix. Having said that, I have not seen a single study that would suggest that the share that renewable energy will have in the total primary energy consumption will be more than, say, 10 percent in the next 20 years. A growth in renewable energy will be dependent not only on technological developments but also on the price of those fossil fuels, and as Dr. Angevine pointed out, the world is in very good shape with respect to the availability of a variety of traditional energy forms. The likelihood is that the prices of those energy forms will remain stable, or perhaps even decline in real terms, which will make it difficult for more expensive forms to penetrate the marketplace. That does raise environmental issues which we have to address, but from at least one perspective, that's good news.

If we were facing a world in which there were substantially higher real energy prices over time, that would mean that we would have to adjust away from energy consumption much more rapidly than is currently the case, and it would reduce the availability of income to spend on other things that we value as a society.

Ms. Tyerman

I agree with Mr. Lyman's comments about the interest in non-renewables internationally; that has been apparent for a long time. But I think we should bear in mind that the situation is not quite so stark as being dependent on one source of oil. Think of the Gulf War; that was a time when you might have expected oil prices to rise, yet because Western countries put some of their reserves of oil on the market, they in fact stabilized the price. So I think that is an example of the ability of the market system to respond to those kinds of crises.

I do not believe that a single source of energy will be dominated by one single feature to which the world will be unable to adjust. I do think that we are moving toward renewables, but from an economic perspective it is clear that that will not happen immediately. So I don't think the future is quite as stark as sometimes we see it; when we say that there is a 30 year supply of a particular energy source available, that refers to proven reserves. As we move closer to the 30 year mark, that time horizon will move further away as we discover more proven reserves, and as other technologies come about.

Brigadier-General George Bell, CISS

Dr. Angevine, I was impressed with the figures you put before us and the fact that the gross picture is such that we have a significant level of world supply for the future. However I was particularly impressed with the fact that when you looked at certain continents, for example Africa, you saw a great maldistribution, such as a limited amount of crude oil, a limited amount of gas, virtually no coal, and an excess capacity of uranium. I wonder how you would consider this maldistribution of resources insofar as it affects stability in the developing areas. There is a similar situation in Latin America to some degree, and I wonder if there is some strategic significance to the data which we have not looked at here in terms of how the world will deal with the problems of the depressed areas. In Africa, for example, people are using up wood for heating. They do not have the kind of use of energy which we have yet, but we are projecting a high use of energy which would presumably require a lot of capital distribution, a lot of building of pipelines, a lot of exploration for a continent such as Africa, and I wonder if you had some views on this.

Dr. Angevine

As I indicated, most of the growth in the demand for energy is going to come from the developing and emerging developed countries, and there are imbalances. With regard to the industrialized countries, as I have indicated, both in the case of natural gas and oil, only 10 percent of the supplies are within those areas, but that of course is another issue.

With regard to the developing countries, there are problems that will have to be addressed. Coal will be used heavily in the developing countries, certainly in China and India. Some of those very heavily populated regions of the world will continue to use coal in a very significant way, and coal share worldwide is unlikely to decline by very much. There are environmental concerns on that score. If we do what we can to ensure that the power generation facilities in the developing world that use coal use the latest, so-called clean coal, technologies, then we will have a lot to be thankful for, but that will be expensive, and it will take a lot of work. It is interesting that Ontario Hydro and Hydro Quebec are involved, as they are now in China, and through mechanisms like that it is hoped that there can be some transfer of the latest technologies.

I am impressed, as you were, when I look at the world balances and see how little in the way of resources there seems to be in some very large areas like Latin America. There is very little uranium and coal indicated as sitting in Latin America, and I cannot help thinking that there may still be a lot of these resources in Latin America which remain to be discovered. The situation in Africa, as in India, will require utilisation of renewable energies; certainly the opportunity for solar is significant for some of those areas. In fact, we are doing a study with an energy research institute in India that is looking at prospects for the Indian electric power sector, and in so doing we are looking at how the current energy mix in India, with its heavy reliance on conventional coal technologies, can be improved upon in the future. We are looking at how renewables and demand-side management, conservation, decentralization of power and other things might improve upon the situation. There are a lot of difficult questions to answer. Certainly we at CERI have not yet looked at some, indeed many, of them in terms of the international issues, and I think that there is a lot of challenging work to be done yet.

Donald Lawson

The Future of the Canadian Nuclear Industry

I am pleased to have the opportunity to participate at this seminar and to speak on "The Future of the Canadian Nuclear Industry".

I have spent my career commercially exploiting the benefits of nuclear technology and I am optimistic about its future prospects. Let me highlight for you the fundamental factors that will drive our industry in the future.

I would like to begin by addressing our need for electricity. I will consider this issue from a global context.

The World Energy Congress, at its meeting in Madrid in 1992, tabled the results of a detailed and comprehensive study conducted by its international team. The team studied three global energy scenarios:

1. The reference case - business as usual with some improved efficiency;

2. The enhanced economic development case - projecting strong worldwide economic growth, particularly in the developing world; and

3. The ecologically driven case - with stronger attention being paid to environmental protection.

Between 1990 and 2020, world energy growth for the three scenarios is expected to be 53 percent, 98 percent, and 29 percent respectively.

Mr. Lawson is President of AECL CANDU, the design engineering and marketing arm of the federal Crown Corporation Atomic Energy of Canada Limited.

The growth of nuclear power over the same period was predicted to be 100 percent, 250 percent, and 75 percent for the three cases.

We can see that regardless of which scenario emerges, there will be a substantial increase in the use of nuclear power in the next 20 to 30 years. This does not mean, however, that we in the nuclear industry can sit back, wait for the business and reap the profits. Our ability as an industry to address a number of key issues will ultimately determine our success.

I would like to take a brief look at these issues:

1. The structural changes in the utility industry;

2. The economics of nuclear power;

3. The financial constraints on the power industry in the developing world;

4. Safety, environmental protection and waste management; and

5. Our ability to develop new products which will satisfy future demand.

The first is structural change in the utility industry. The worldwide electrical utility industry is changing rapidly. Around the world, utilities are being privatized. Power plants are being built by Independent Power Producers (IPPs) and Non-Utility Generators (NUGs). Vendors are being asked to deliver their product under BOT (Build, own and transfer), BOOT (build, own, operate and transfer) and ROT (rehabilitate, own and transfer) schemes. Governments are mandating access to transmission lines. Utilities are breaking up their generation, transmission, and retail distribution segments into separate profit centres, as is the case with Ontario Hydro.

Could shopping for electricity be just a "1-800" number away? Deregulation has made bargain hunters out of once-captive customers in markets like long-distance telecommunications, natural gas and trucking. Is electricity next?

In this highly competitive environment, utilities with high-cost generation may eventually find it difficult to stay in business. The challenge for the nuclear power industry will be to demonstrate that it can generate electricity at rates that enable plant owners to stay competitive.

This leads us to the next topic: the economic viability of our product. I am happy to report that the nuclear power industry, and AECL CANDU in particular, have been quite successful in developing and delivering an economically viable product. At the same time, it is somewhat disheartening that we are unable fully to convince the public at large of this fact.

The levelized unit energy cost (LUEC) is the universally accepted method of determining the costs of producing electricity for the lifetime of the plant. It is the preferred unit of measurement by the International Atomic Energy Agency, the OECD and the World Bank. It takes the total lifetime discounted costs of electricity production, including building, operating, decommissioning and waste fuel storage and divides this by the total discounted lifetime production to arrive at a cost per kilowatt hour.

The most recent data submitted to the OECD in December of 1992 shows that, for reference plants built in central Canada, CANDU nuclear power plants can produce electricity at 3.27 cents per kilowatt hour, while coal is about 10 percent more expensive at 3.58 cents per kilowatt hour. Ontario Hydro's 1992 Annual Report records the cost of electricity per kilowatt hour: for 1992 the cost of a fossil-fired plant cost Ontario Hydro 5.037 cents per kilowatt hour, and nuclear cost 4.824 cents, and that was not even a particularly good year for nuclear operations in Ontario.

You heard this morning Mr. Strong quoting a figure of $14 billion for the nuclear generating station at Darlington. If you take that $14 billion and convert it into US dollars and divide it by the 880 megawatts of each of the four units of Darlington you arrive at an installed capital cost of $2,980 (US) per kilowatt. If you look at the data submitted by Korea to the OECD agencies, the cost of a CANDU unit that we are now building in Korea is $1,810 (US) per kilowatt. Why is there such a big disparity? If we build plants here in Ontario in the same way as we are doing in Korea, why does it cost so much more here? I should add that we are building them to the same standards in Korea; these are international standards and the safety standards are just the same in both plants.

The data submitted by the Koreans to the OECD is very interesting, as Korea is the only country in the world where both CANDU plants and American pressurized water reactors (PWRs) are in operation virtually side by side. The Korean data shows that CANDU plants are producing electricity at 3.89 cents per kilowatt hour, PWRs are about 10 percent more expensive at 4.35 cents , with coal 10 percent more expensive than PWRs at 4.73 cents per kilowatt hour. We are less expensive than our nuclear competitors, not because we have less concrete and steel but because we can build faster and the more expensive items are paid for later in construction. Hence the interest costs on the construction are less.

The next issue I would like to address concerns the financial constraints our industry faces. According to the World Energy Congress, at least 85 percent of the anticipated increase in global energy consumption over the next few decades is expected to occur in the developing world as a result of efforts to alleviate poverty and improve material progress. It is clear that a growing segment of the business for the electrical power generation product vendors will be in the developing world and newly industrialized countries. The World Bank estimates that $60 billion a year will be needed to finance this growth at the beginning of the 1990s, increasing to $110 billion by the end of this decade.

Unfortunately, the amount of export financing available from Canada is and will continue to be limited. Therefore, in order to access the resources of the international financial community to win sales, we need to limit the Canadian content of our future projects, and to form international partnerships and alliances. Under these conditions it is apparent that the Canadian nuclear industry will need to accept the fact that a piece of the pie is better than no pie at all.

Next I would like to turn to the issues of safety, environmental protection and waste management. All of the CANDUs that we have supplied anywhere have been acceptable both to Canadian regulations and the regulations of the countries in which they have been installed and that still holds true. For example, with Wolsong 2, 3 and 4, CANDU met all the requirements for licensing in both Canada and Korea, the latter having licensed both PWR and CANDU systems.

Part of CANDU's licensing acceptability is its approach to safety. CANDU incorporates "defence-in-depth" design. Multiple boundaries and independent shutdown systems are built into the design. This advanced approach is proven with decades of reliability data that reflects the importance of safety designs.

Of note is the fact that CANDU has established an excellent long-term history of minimizing radiation doses to operating staff. This has contributed to ease of plant maintenance which in turn has contributed to better operating reliability and lower operating costs. In practice radiation doses approach one percent of the regulatory limit.

I recognize that radiation concerns people. Let us try to put it in perspective. If you are exposed to 500,000 millirems of radiation, you have a 50:50 chance of dying from the effect. Below 200,000 there seem to be no discernable immediate effects.

We all live in atomic radiation from nature. Every second you and I are being struck by about 15,000 sub-atomic particles travelling at about 100,000 miles/sec. Each has some chance of hitting a cell and damaging it. However the chance is so low that only one-half of one percent of all cancers are attributed to natural radiation. In Canada, the average natural background radiation is 80 millirems. If you live in Banff, the skiing may be good but the background radiation is twice the Canadian average -- due to altitude and rocks. Living just outside a nuclear plant gives 0.003 millirems from the plant; only a tiny fraction of natural background levels. The often-cited Three Mile Island accident gave off only 1.5 millirems to the people downwind of the plant, for a short period of time, again, only a small fraction of natural background levels. It is well worth noting that airline crews are exposed to about the same radiation levels as the average nuclear workers.

Now we can delve into the issue of environmental protection. To produce the same amount of electricity, nuclear uses less land, less fuel and produces less waste than coal. It is a combustion-free process, so we get none of the ash, carbon dioxide, sulphur dioxide and nitrous oxide emissions released by our fossil-based competition.

It is interesting to note the sources of carbon dioxide in the atmosphere in Canada. Surprisingly, gas dominates. It is estimated that natural gas accounts for 140 million tonnes of carbon dioxide emissions each year, with coal running a distant second at 85 million tonnes; yet there is a popular notion that gas is clean and does not contribute to greenhouse gases. Nuclear energy emits no carbon dioxide into the atmosphere.

I know that many people ask "But aren't nuclear wastes a pollution?" The answer is no. The overall philosophy is to provide the interim storage at the reactor site followed by permanent disposal underground in geologically stable formations. The Canadian and Ontario governments agreed in 1978 to cooperate in the development of technologies for the safe permanent disposal of nuclear waste. The basic R&D phase of this program has now been completed and the findings and recommendations are currently undergoing an exhaustive, independent review by the Federal Environmental Assessment Review Organization with full public participation at every stage.

The concept is simple. Our design is very similar to what nature did with the original ore. Fuel will be stored in metal canisters seal-welded together, in bentonite clay hulls in solid granite rock. This is almost an exact parallel of what nature did with the ores; the rich deposits in Saskatchewan, for example, were impossible to detect from the surface, and they have been there for billions of years. If we use the same approach as nature, we will have the answer to nuclear waste.

Let me turn to the issue of product development. While I highlighted some of the key issues facing our industry and demonstrated to you how we plan to address them, I do not want to leave you with the impression that our product has reached the final stages of its development. At AECL, if we are to continue to succeed in the international marketplace, we must continuously gauge market conditions, monitor technological breakthroughs and develop products that will meet the needs of tomorrow's customer.

We must continue to design safe plants which can be built more quickly and cheaply if we are to achieve our goal of securing one quarter of the new nuclear orders worldwide. In our marketplace, the competition is getting fiercer. Coal is going down in price, gas fired combined cycle units offer cheap power. We have to look continuously to reduce our costs and be more competitive.

The most recent IAEA data shows that CANDU plants account for just over seven percent of all nuclear units in service around the world. There are 12 CANDU units under construction out of a total of 72 units under construction worldwide. Add in the two units we recently sold to Korea and you can see that CANDUs account for over 15 percent of total units under construction.

AECL is not far from reaching its goal of one-quarter of the world market. This is a tremendous achievement when you consider the size of our manufacturing capability and the special limitations we have in Canada such as export financing mentioned earlier.

In the short term it appears that there will be little requirement for additional plants in Canada. However in the Pacific Rim, countries like Indonesia, and Thailand and China project electricity growth at 10 to 15 percent a year. This is where we have the greatest opportunities for Canadian technology.

Our continued success will bring with it a significant number of high-tech jobs for Canada which will continue to fuel the Canadian economy.

Forum

Col. Martin, National Defence College

You discussed nuclear and coal, but not hydroelectricity. Could you comment on hydro please?

Mr. Lawson

If you would like me to quote the figures on hydro costs, I can quote them. They are by far the lowest. They came in last year at 1.05 cents per kilowatt hour. That is largely because these hydro plants are very old plants and the capital cost has been written off. There are plants in this province that are nearly 100 years old and have been well written off.

We have looked at the economics of CANDU versus some of the new hydro developments and we believe we are neck and neck in price when the costs of transmission from remote hydro sites to the load centres are taken into account. We are about on the same basis there.

One other point that is often overlooked is that hydro plants do have their own environmental problems. Look, for example, at the Three Gorges plant in China. As I understand it, it is going to displace 1.5 million people -- that is an enormous environmental change for those people. Also, if you look in the northern rivers, the actual building of the dams disturbs the geology; disturbing the geology releases a lot of natural mercury from the ground. So there are problems up in the James Bay area with high levels of mercury in the fish, as a result of hydro-electric projects. I also understand that methane (a greenhouse gas) is produced as a result of vegetation which rots due to flooding of large areas.

So I think that in the future we can compete there. But if I go to the World Energy Congress figures, they also predict significant development in hydro in various parts in the world. It is interesting to remember that 20 years ago people were saying that all of the main rivers had been used and that there was little remaining hydroelectric potential. This underlines the fact that making predictions in this business is quite tough and that they can easily be wrong.

Brigadier-General Michael Webber, CISS

Given that the public concern about nuclear waste is one of the biggest weapons in the anti-nuclear arsenal, your remark about the possibility of using thorium interests me because of the very, very diminished waste product associated with it. Can you tell us anything about the availability of thorium in Canada and in other areas of the world, and whether or not in concept it could be an economical alternative?

Mr. Lawson

Thorium is fairly widely distributed around the world. There are some countries with more thorium than others; I think India has a particularly large supply of thorium, and so has Turkey. We are bidding in Turkey at present, and the people there are very interested in that. I believe that there are thorium deposits in Alberta, but I am not absolutely sure of that. Of course with a very rich uranium resource it is probable that the cost of the thorium cycle would be higher; that remains to be studied.

One of the points that has been made in the course of our presentations in Europe is that people around the world are looking at advanced reactors, and they are taking on various new approaches. Nuclear research for improving safety to reduce the risk of death in a nuclear plant costs something like $100 million of R&D per person; yet you could get that same effect by spending $100,000 on medical research. So there is a huge disparity there. So while the world at large has developed a programme for looking at advanced reactors, what the Europeans are telling us is that surely that is not addressing the real problem. The real problem concerns the wastes from the reactors, rather than the safety of the reactors themselves. Other than the Chernobyl-type reactor, the other designs used around the world have proven to be basically safe.

The CANDU reactor was originally designed as a kind of neutron efficient reactor. It can burn a variety of fuels because it is so efficient in the use of neutrons, and so in some ways it can be called a nuclear garbage burner. The thorium cycle is one of several cycles we can use. Another approach is to burn actinides which are some of the waste products from the current reactors and we can generate energy that way and reduce the long-life fission products at the same time.

I was really dangling this as a carrot. I believe it is a very valid one, one on which we have done some research in the past and will continue in the future. India has in fact loaded a CANDU reactor with thorium and is running it now on thorium, but as we have no association with that country on this matter, we are not sure of what the actual details are.

Mr. Nixon

Mr. Strong said this morning that we have about two decades during which to come to grips with this energy concern, not so much because of the supply issue as because of the environmental issue. What are your views on how we in North America, and particularly the United States, are going to go about restructuring the whole energy infrastructure, including the transportation sector? How can it be accomplished in two decades, when you consider that it takes five years to build a plant and it takes about 15 years from the time the application is made until the time that it is approved?

Mr. Lawson

My simple answer is that I don't know what sort of crisis it is going to take to make those changes occur. In the US for at least the last decade there has been talk about revising the nuclear regulations, and that has really only slowly and very painfully occurred, I think largely because it is in a position somewhat similar to ours. The USA has adequate generating capacity at present and now some people are saying that the nuclear industry is dead while others say it is not. While there is no nuclear construction going on right now in the US, the nuclear business is good. Currently there are some 110 or 111 nuclear power plants generating something like 20 percent of the electricity of the US and clearly there are business opportunities in servicing and maintaining that, so it depends on how you look at it.

I think it is going to take some sort of crisis to produce action. It is interesting to see other countries around the world looking at this and we take some heart from that. If you focus mainly on programmes in Europe you would say the nuclear industry is dead; there is nothing going on in Germany; France is building slowly. France has a nice programme; it can sit back and build power plants and while everyone else's regulatory system is getting into trouble, the French just sell electricity here, there and everywhere. The electricity industry in the UK is chaotic, the nuclear industry is even more chaotic, so what is happening is that 2,000 megawatts of French nuclear electricity is being sold into the UK continuously. Italy stopped its nuclear programme and now 20 percent of its electricity comes from France's nuclear capability. So is that a political decision or not? France is also selling to other countries of Europe, for example, Spain and Portugal.

In North America you will get the answer I just gave -- the nuclear industry is dead. In the Pacific, however, the dominant economy, Japan, is building more nuclear power plants; Taiwan is looking at ordering more units -- one-third of their electricity comes from nuclear. We are busy in Korea, where the economy has clearly benefited from the use of nuclear. Korea has no coal, gas, or oil of its own and half of its electricity comes from nuclear. So the countries that are following that pattern have obviously looked to Japan's example, and even those countries that have energy resources of their own, such as Taiwan and China and Indonesia are all looking at joining the nuclear club. Now China has two nuclear power plants in operation, it is another potential market for us. But when you go there you see the whole national infrastructure being centred around new railway lines built to take coal from the north to the power centres in the south.

The political regulations in certain countries have to be changed. I do not think it needs to take 15 years -- we can get environmental approval, we can get up-front licensing and we can get the plant going more quickly. One of the reasons why Darlington was expensive was that the people at Ontario

Hydro did not know whether they could get a license to operate it before they completely finished it; and there was the interest on $14 billion building day by day. We are now working with the Atomic Energy Control Board, the nuclear agency here in Canada, to try to get up-front licensing. Before making a financial commitment, you need to make sure that you have a license so that when you spend the money you can use it as an effective asset.

I really do not know the complete answer to your question, but in part, we will have to apply a lot of pressure to try and change the regulatory climate.

Robert Pines

Energy Security and the Free Market

Introduction

I am a conservative Republican New York businessman. Between September 1988 and January 1993 I was a conservative Republican Washington bureaucrat. It will therefore come as no surprise that this paper will speak kindly of the roles of the free market and international cooperation in the histories of the three NAFTA countries. My basic argument is that energy security can only come through economic freedom.

NEP

In the case of Canada, the starting point could well be the late unlamented National Energy Programme. Prime Minister Pierre Trudeau introduced this in 1980 with the high minded declared purpose of Canadianizing the energy industry and insuring Canada's self-sufficiency in energy.

In Peter Brimelow's[1] formulation, the NEP was a blow to American oil companies in Canada. As with Canadian companies, Ottawa was intervening to "back in" to a part ownership of their discoveries, and to expropriate through royalties and taxes the so-called windfall profits they were about to receive because they had the foresight to acquire assets whose prices were rising.

Mr. Pines is President of Pines Venture Capital Corporation and former US Deputy Assistant Secretary of State

From the Alberta government's standpoint, the NEP was Ottawa muscling into its revenue sources. From the oil industry's standpoint, the NEP was an anchor dragging down Canadian oil production.

Dr. Charles Doran[2] of the Center of Canadian Studies at Johns Hopkins University presented at the time a trenchant analysis of the NEP, stating,

> Ottawa thought it needed to defend the interests of central Canadian consumers and industrial users, and pursued this goal under the disguise of 'equity'.

The basic error of the NEP was its assumption of indefinitely rising prices. My case, not unlike that of the "Jurassic Park" film, is that if not this error, some other would have been made by the human mind attempting to substitute itself for the infinite complexities of nature, in this case, the free market.

The NEP is now dead and gone. Removing its shackles from your country's superb oil industry has resulted in gains for all -- greater production, lower prices, more supply for all Canadians, and even, yes, more revenue for Ottawa to dispense in its wisdom.

NAFTA

I turn to the Free Trade Agreement. The salient apposite section is Article 904. This is the "proportionality" or "security of supply" clause. Canada committed therein, in case of crisis, to cut oil and gas exports to the USA by no greater a percentage than energy supplies were reduced for its domestic market.

Canada's negotiators in 1987 appeared to have to be dragged kicking and screaming to accept this clause. However a Canadian representative told a former State Department colleague of mine that quite a bit of theatre was present -- that it was widely realized that Canada would profit from *security of market* as much as America from *security of supply*.

The happy result for Canada has been many long-term contracts with American independent power projects. Buyers have indicated they would never have entered into contracts as long as 20 years without the indispensable assurance of Article 904.

Of even broader long-term value to Canada, since FTA, the Federal Energy Regulatory Commission has increasingly come to refer to an integrated North American Energy Market, and grant national treatment for Canadian resources.

In NAFTA negotiations the Mexicans, following Article 27 of their constitution, refused a proportionality clause similar to 904. It was dismaying to see the Canadian negotiators taking careful aim at their own feet by trying to abrogate the original 904, and thus severely damage their own industry's long-term contract prospects. One may often also apply to American bureaucrats characterizing the Bourbon monarchs: *rien appris, rien oublié.*

Due note must of course also be taken of the Liberal Party Red Book, and post-election pronouncements of the prime minister designate. Entirely apart from the good sense of Mr. Chretien, the following must be pointed out: Canada is a member of the International Energy Association. Even if by some misguided *legerdemain* Canada were to escape its FTA obligation, in case of crisis its obligation to make up for shortfalls would, under IEA, exceed that under FTA.

The United States is not without fault. For example, implementation of mandatory oil import quotas between 1958 and 1973 was rightly resented by many Canadians. However, this and other petty irritants did not compare to the NEP or Mexican constitutional structures. Nevertheless we escaped our own brush with destructive proto-socialism with President Carter's harebrained scheme, grandiosely styled the Moral Equivalent of War (MEOW).

It must once again be thankfully noted that the free market washed away this monstrosity by rectifying higher prices through conservation, augmented production and other natural adjustments. Similarly, in my country the freeing of gas prices resulted, after an initial spike, in sharply reduced prices.

Mexico is of course the hard case. Every Mexican child with his first *tortilla* imbibes the national wail about being "so far from God, so close to the United States". Article 27 of the Mexican constitution, defining oil as the national patrimony, essentially bars private activity in the basic petroleum industry.

NAFTA could not abolish this provision, so rooted in the Mexican psyche and so destructive to the well-being of that potentially prosperous country. However, the impact of the clause has been dented somewhat.

The NAFTA accord opens most petrochemicals in Mexico to foreign investment, permits electricity production, authorizes direct national gas sales between US and Canadian suppliers and Mexican customers, and allows Pemex to pay "performance" bonuses to successful oil exploration firms.

As noted, the agreement still bars foreign ownership of Mexican oil reserves. Observers in the Texas-focused oil patch view the bonus provision as an important step toward Mexico's entering into "risk contracts" in a few years, although nobody is saying this too loudly.

An important breakthrough lies in greater opportunities for US and Canadian companies to increase sales to Pemex and the Federal Electricity Commission, which have long followed a "buy-Mexico" policy. These two energy monopolies, whose purchases exceed (US) $8 billion annually, must expose 50 percent of these acquisitions to open bidding by North American suppliers during the first year of the accord. The percentage jumps to 70 percent in the fifth year and almost 100 percent after nine years.

Tariffs on oil field equipment will also be phased out. American trade associations believe that sales of goods and services to Mexico's energy sector will increase by (US) $1 billion or more the first year that NAFTA takes effect.

This completes my thesis on the assigned topic of continental political and diplomatic issues. Time limits the discussion of other forms of energy, other successes and omissions in the FTA, and such important questions as environmental concerns.

Of course, more perils lurk in the further reaches of the global village.

"Security Margin"

The objective of energy security, in Daniel Yergin's[3] words, is to assure adequate supplies of energy at reasonable prices and in ways that do not jeopardize major national values and objectives.

Yergin[4] introduces the concept of "security margin" -- an excess of supply over demand sufficient to cushion sudden energy shocks. Typically the current world situation yields good news and bad news.

OPEC's share of the world oil market fell from 63 percent in 1972 (excluding the former Soviet Union) to 38 percent in 1985.

Soviet production in 1988 stood at 12.5 million barrels per day (11.5 million from Russia). Today, Russian production is a mere seven million. An investment on the order of $50 billion between now and 2000 is needed merely to stabilize the present level; otherwise Russian output could fall as low as 4 million barrels per day.

Iraq's substantial production waits on the sidelines to join the other supplying countries. However, oil demand is increasing as well. By early the next decade, Asia is expected to consume more than North America.

In the 1980s the world oil market operated at an average 80 percent capacity. Not even factoring in Iraq it is up to an ominous 92 percent.

What to do? Obviously it is necessary to facilitate the free flow of investment capital to restore the once ample production of the former Soviet Union. However the nationalist opposition there poses a problem reminiscent of Mexico.

On our side the security margin must be augmented by such expedients as conservation, the Strategic Petroleum Reserve and the tax laws encouraging exploration.

Conclusion

However, to return to my main theme, the most promising path to energy security lies in allowing free competition worldwide and investment at a reasonable return set by the market and untrammelled by governments.

Notes

1. Brimelow, "The Patriot Game," 1986.
2. Doran, "Forgotten Partnership", 1984.
3. Yergin, "Energy Security in the 1990s", in Foreign Affairs, 1988.
4. Stanislow and Yergin, "Oil: Reopening the Door", in Foreign Affairs, 1993.

John Purdie

The Growing Strategic Importance
of Middle Eastern Oil

Introduction

My introduction to the topic of fossil fuel reserves occurred over 30 years ago while I was doing research on the chemical constitution of coal. One book I read stated that the reserves of coal in the world were sufficient for a thousand years. It continued by pointing out that the world's oil reserves were sufficient for about 25 years. The book then proceeded to reassure readers by explaining that the oil reserve was a moving 25 years; each year sufficient reserves for another year were discovered so that the total reserve stayed more or less constant. Within its limited time frame, the book was correct. The oil reserves kept moving. In fact, they have moved to the ends of the earth. Today most areas of the globe have been explored to a greater or lesser extent. At present there are reserves for over 25 years.

There is no doubt that more oil fields will be discovered, but it has become increasingly difficult to keep up with the huge demand for conventional oil, 67 million barrels per day. To put it in perspective, consider the following: if all the oil from the Hibernia oilfield off Newfoundland could be used to meet the world demand, it would be sufficient for only ten days. The Prudhoe Bay oilfield in Alaska is much larger. It belongs in the class referred to as super-giant oil fields and could supply the world for about six months.

Dr. Purdie is a Scientific and Technical Analyst at National Defence Headquarters.

Oil: A Strategic Commodity

Oil is the leading energy source of the world, accounting for approximately 40 percent of the total (see Table 1). Unfortunately, the earth's reserves of oil are relatively limited and unevenly distributed. The most accessible sources of oil have already been depleted in many countries.

At the current rate of use, 24 billion barrels per year, the conventional oil reserves in most areas of the world will be depleted over the next 30 years. I should point out that when I refer to an oil reserve as being depleted it does not imply totally exhausted. It means that the productive capacity using conventional extraction methods has decreased to a very low level. Enhanced oil recovery techniques can be used to increase the yield substantially in oil-fields that have not already been abandoned, but at a much higher cost. Also, since this analysis is based on the current rate of use, increased conservation in the industrial countries could lead to a decrease in consumption. Against that, however, is the expectation that the developing countries will increase their demand for oil significantly.

The main exception to the anticipated depletion of oil reserves during the next 30 years is the Middle East, where reserves are estimated to be about 65 percent of the total world reserves (see Table 2). Thus, as current oil fields are depleted or as production decreases, an increasing proportion of the oil will have to come from the Middle East, or to be more precise, the countries around the Persian Gulf. This trend is already in progress. In fact, as one US energy expert pointed out in 1990 prior to the Gulf War, overdependence on oil from the Middle East has created foreign policy dilemmas for the United States and a risk of war.

The effect of declining oil reserves is best demonstrated graphically. Figure 1 shows the remaining oil reserves at ten year intervals. After 30 years the principal region with large oil reserves is the Middle East. Latin America also has a significant amount remaining. However, the chart is rather theoretical. Within the next 30 years, some of the alternative energy sources will probably be developed. Also, the effect of burning fossil fuels on the climate will become clearer and may affect energy choices.

Most OECD countries now maintain a six month stock of oil. Any major disruption in the supply of Middle Eastern oil that extends beyond six months would have severe economic impacts, not only on the industrial world, but also on the developing countries. This situation will continue until such time as alternative energy supplies are developed to decrease the dependence on oil from the Persian Gulf region. These could be other energy sources, or unconventional oil. However, any of the available options would require a massive investment in facilities and infrastructure which would take many years to put in place.

The Energy Alternatives

What are the alternatives to conventional oil? So-called "unconventional" oil can be obtained from other hydrocarbon sources. The most important of these is bitumen which occurs in the tar sands in Alberta and as extra heavy oil in Venezuela. Unconventional oil is already being extracted from these sources on a small scale. Shale oil could also be used as a source but the cost of extraction is prohibitive at the present time. Coal could be converted into oil but the economics of this process are unattractive at present. Also, the resulting oil could not be used as a direct substitute for conventional oil in the petrochemical industry.

The alternatives to oil also have limitations. Reserves of natural gas are similar to those of oil although the global distribution is more even. Thus a shift from oil to natural gas would simply result in a more rapid depletion of the latter. Reserves of coal are much greater than those of oil or gas and are sufficient for hundreds of years at the current rate of use. Unfortunately, burning coal to produce energy is more harmful to the environment.

Nuclear power has fallen into disfavour in many countries due to rising costs and concerns about safety. The introduction of inherently safe and diversion proof reactors may allay these fears but it is doubtful that nuclear reactors will be built in sufficient numbers to substitute for oil as the supply dwindles in the first half of the next century. Nuclear fusion holds the promise of abundant energy but it is still at the research stage. It is estimated that this source of energy will not be available until after the middle of the next century, too distant to affect the oil equation. Although solar energy is abundant, harnessing it on a scale sufficient to meet current energy demands would be difficult and expensive.

United States Concerns

I believe it is also important to examine the situation from the point of view of the United States. From 1945 until 1990 the predominant feature of US defence policy was containment of the Soviet Union and its allies. The demise of the Warsaw Pact followed closely by the breakup of the Soviet Union has undoubtedly resulted in a major rethinking of US foreign policy and, more particularly, defence priorities. It is highly likely that an issue of growing importance, from a US perspective, is energy, especially the continuing availability of conventional oil.

Thus, it can be assumed that the United States has conducted detailed analyses of the situation, both by government and under contract. Such analyses could identify and explore a broad range of aspects and options. It is reasonable to deduce that a major conclusion is that protection of friendly governments of oil exporting states in the Middle East is imperative. Equally important is the protection of the oil transportation system. The most important oil exporting region in the world is the Persian Gulf and the principal exporter is Saudi Arabia. As can be seen in Table 3, several of the adjacent Arab states are also major oil producers. This table lists the populations of the oil producing countries in the Persian Gulf. It is noteworthy that some of the countries with very large oil reserves have small populations and therefore a limited ability to defend themselves, for example, the United Arab Emirates, with 2.5 million people, and Kuwait, with 1.4 million.

Needless to say, the strategic importance of Middle Eastern oil is not lost on the countries in the region. In fact, that may have been the principal motive behind Iraq's invasion of Kuwait in 1990. It is also noteworthy that Iran has repeatedly stated that the military forces of Western countries should leave the Persian Gulf and the Middle East.

Implications for Canada

The oil outlook appears less critical for Canada. Although most of our conventional oil reserves will be depleted early in the next century, the tar sands of Alberta could yield an estimated 300 billion barrels of oil, more than the current reserves of Saudi Arabia. Thus, Canada could become a major supplier on the world market as the reserves of conventional oil decrease in the course of the next century. As a member of the International Energy Agency, Canada has agreed to provide oil to other OECD countries during emergencies. However, there is no long-term commitment to supply oil to these countries.

Many other industrial countries, however, are in a similar or worse situation than the United States. The UK, for example, has passed the peak of production from its oil fields in the North Sea. France, Italy, Germany and Japan do not have significant domestic supplies of oil. Thus, it can be anticipated that if the US takes the lead in providing military assistance to friendly oil producing countries in the Middle East during a crisis, several of Canada's allies will do likewise.

The vital question is, will Canada get involved? Given its role in the Western world, Canada may feel obliged to contribute forces, even if it is not under United Nations auspices. Any crisis that causes severe economic disruption in the industrial countries will have a major impact on Canada, regardless of our oil reserves. Also, it is important to bear in mind the defence concerns of our allies, particularly the United States. Canada's reaction will probably depend on many factors such as, for example, the nature of the crisis, the response, the countries involved, the threat to economic stability, and so on. Subtle pressure from some of our allies may also be a consideration.

Conclusions

Based on this analysis the principal conclusions are:

–   As current oil fields are depleted or as production decreases over the next 30 years, an increasing proportion of the conventional oil used in the world will have to come from the Middle East.

–   Disruptions of Middle Eastern oil supplies that extend beyond six months would cause severe damage to the economies of the industrial and developing countries. The risk of this occurring will remain until alternative energy supplies are developed.

–   The growing strategic importance of the Middle East as a source of conventional oil could lead to new conflicts in that area. The US and its allies will probably become involved if friendly oil-producing countries such as Saudi Arabia are threatened. Canada may feel obliged to join its allies in such a conflict.

That concludes my brief look at this complex and intriguing subject. I will add that all of the data I have used comes from open sources.

Table 1: Global Energy Consumption

Oil	39%
Coal	30%
Natural gas	20%
Hydroelectric	7%
Nuclear	5%

Table 2: World Oil Reserves by Region

Region	Reserves (Billion barrels)	Percentage	Depletion (Years)
Middle East	662	66	104
Latin America	123	13	51
FSU and E. Europe	59	6	18
Africa	62	6	27
Australasia	45	4	19
North America	30	3	9
Western Europe	16	2	10
Canada	5	0.5	9

Table 3: Middle East: Oil Reserves and Populations

Country	Oil Reserves (Billion barrels)	Population (Million)
Saudi Arabia	257.8	17.0
Iraq	100	18.5
United Arab Emirates	98.9	2.5
Kuwait	94.1	1.4
Iran	92.9	61.2
Qatar	3.7	0.5
Oman	4.3	1.6

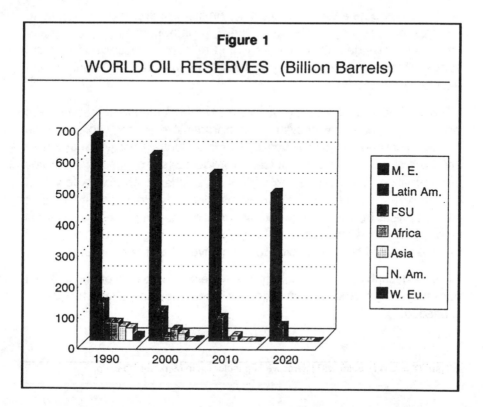

Figure 1

WORLD OIL RESERVES   (Billion Barrels)

████████

William D'Silva

Meeting the Challenge: CEMaC:
A Newly Developed Canadian Central Energy
Management and Control System

We have come here today to examine, brainstorm and plan strategies to meet a series of energy challenges. One of the important strategies in meeting these challenges is that of energy and resource conservation. The old adage, "A penny saved is a penny earned" holds true, as well, for energy and related resources.

Tertec, TerStar and VIC, a group of related high technology companies would like to offer an innovative, comprehensive strategy for resource management and conservation called CEMaC, Central Energy Management and Control. It is a mass communication product based on the new economy of information. The heart of the CEMaC is a little green box, a low cost electronic transponder which, when installed in residences and offices, records pulses from water, gas and electrical meters, manages and controls loads, and forms the basis of future services ranging from electronic newspapers and home shopping to interactive TV and remote education.

Before describing the technology in any detail, and based on the fact that necessity is the mother of all inventions, it is necessary to outline why CEMaC is needed.

William D'Silva is Director, VIC Interactive Technologies in Markham, Ontario.

In North America, public utilities have for some time been at the forefront of the search for ways to conserve. But once a utility delivers energy or water to the homes or offices of its customers, it loses control over how much is used and when -- and in many cases, so do its customers. If consumers do not even know how much is being consumed, then how can they conserve?

For example, enormous loads are placed on distribution systems when residents of a community arrive home from work -- and all use utility resources at the same time. Although all utilities are ready to meet such a peak demand, that demand may occur for only a few hours each month. And, for whatever reason, should the demand be exceeded, then the utility's customers might experience low water pressure, electrical brownouts or even blackouts.

The traditional solution to this problem has been to build more energy generating facilities but, unfortunately, that can often result in a dramatic impact on the environment, not to mention the high costs. In addition, utilities are looking for solutions to meter reading problems which result from "by appointment only" readings, mail back cards, extended intervals between meter readings, consumption estimates, and other situations.

Consider the savings in terms of new plant construction alone! In his talk this morning Mr. Strong indicated price tags of between $3.5 and $14 billion.

The CEMaC is one strategic answer to these and other related problems.

What is the CEMaC?

The CEMaC, to public utility customers, is nothing more than a small green box conveniently located in their homes and linked to their gas, water, electricity meters and switchable devices. But to the utilities themselves, it is a new and direct data communications link to their equipment inside the homes of their customers. The CEMaC gathers data from the meters and transmits it to a central computer, giving utilities fast real-time access to information not only on the amount of energy used, but also on when it was used (Time of Use Readings). The CEMaC also permits utilities to transmit data via a central computer to each green box. This in turn means the utility can regulate supply instantly or according to programmed instructions, turn power on or off to special devices (such as water heaters) in individual homes -- all totally transparent to the customer.

What is the big picture?

CEMaC requires no major new installation to operate. It makes use of existing two-way communication capabilities, sending its data via co-axial cables, power lines, telephone lines, or radio waves.

Where cable TV companies operate, CEMaC can efficiently utilize a small portion of the wide bandwidth available on existing co-axial cables already used to transmit audio and video television signals. CEMaC uses a small fraction of the total capacity of the coaxial cable to transmit data to and from the green boxes installed in each home.

A CEMaC computer located centrally at the cable company's "head end" is the hub of the system. Through it, the CEMaC transponders send their data to the utilities and in turn the utilities transmit their instructions to the transponders.

The entire CEMaC system is totally transparent to cable TV customers. It does not affect their television picture or the cost of their cable service. But it does have the potential to affect the cost of their energy and water beneficially.

Is the CEMaC flexible?

Data can be flexibly transmitted via coaxial cable, telephone lines, power lines, or radio waves -- in any combination. Thus, different installation topologies may be easily accommodated. It is designed modularly and can grow by adding options and modules that will interface with other systems like Smart Houses. Add-ons like the ability to monitor energy consumption on your TV or on LCD displays are under development.

Who derives benefits from the CEMaC?

CEMaC offers clear benefits to utilities and their customers, and to the environment.

CEMaC allows utilities to handle load-shedding on a real-time or pre-programmed basis, and it permits utilities to read meters accurately on a real time basis -- at any time. Also, with "Time of Use" rates, CEMaC gives utility customers an option to exercise some control over their energy costs.

Load-shedding can reduce peak period demand. With the agreement of energy consumers, each green box can deactivate selected appliances (such as water heaters) for short periods to reduce energy consumption during times of peak demand. The CEMaC system can be programmed for each individual home and for each controlled appliance.

Load-shedding can be further encouraged by offering customers lower rates for off-peak energy usage -- in much the same way that telephone companies charge less for long-distance calls made after certain hours. CEMaC provides public utilities the technology to allow them to offer their customers special "Time of Use" energy rates, because the Green Boxes can record and report the amount of energy used and the time of its consumption.

This same technology makes it possible for utilities to develop accurate load profiles for any customer, or any group of customers. As a result, utilities will have more control over the loads on their systems, and they will also enjoy improved buying power.

In addition, following power outages, utilities can use CEMaC's cold load pick-up capabilities to stagger power returning to the controlled device on the system, thus avoiding huge power surges.

Benefits for the Environment

Obviously, CEMaC's biggest contribution to the environment is the ability to offer everyone more efficient use of energy. But there is a host of other important environmental advantages.

With CEMaC, utilities will have more control over their energy supply. They will therefore be able to use existing energy generation and distribution facilities more efficiently. There will be less need for new plant construction -- and consequently less negative impact on the environment.

In Conclusion

The CEMaC has been tried and tested by Ontario Hydro for over two years. It is recommended to all utilities. The Ontario Ministry of Energy through the EnerSearch program participated in the development of the current CEMaC system. In this day where convergence and interactive TV are the buzzwords, the CEMaC is a mass communications product that is here today.

As a result of the successful field trials with Ontario Hydro, we are now in the process of evaluating strategic partners to take the CEMaC to large scale implementation.

Although the use of the CEMaC thus far has been for energy and resource management, the system is truly universal. Its other capabilities and features are constantly being researched and developed.

We have assembled here today to brainstorm strategies to meet the energy challenges of the 21st century. We have one solution, in the form of the CEMaC, to meet those challenges today.

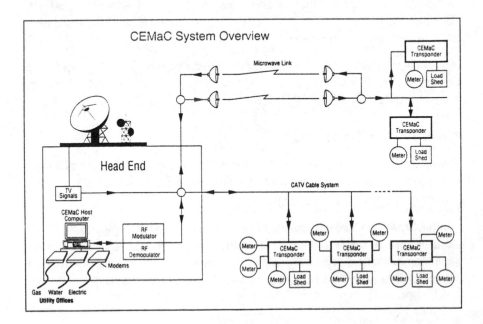

Donald McIvor

Emerging Energy Technologies

I appreciate having the opportunity to take part in this discussion about how Canada will deal with its energy future. Few subjects are as important to sovereign nations as the security and cost of their energy supplies and thus the invitation to take part in this deliberation is very gratifying.

No economy can perform without energy. The economies of the so-called developed nations would regress to the levels of about 250 years ago without the energy supplied by oil, gas, coal and electricity. Thus, the question of how Canada will deal with its energy future is worthy of the most careful consideration.

The subject of how nations deal with their energy supplies is complex in and of itself. Over the past 35 years or so, it has become much more complex due to a growing realization that economic growth must be accompanied by care for the natural environment. Since the production and consumption of energy in itself can have an effect on the natural environment, this has overlain a further complexity on the subject.

I have been asked to address the subject of emerging energy technologies, a subject which raises two very important questions. First, can emerging technologies be made economic enough to compete in the market with conventional sources, which are very cheap because they are in surplus and which get cheaper by means of continued technological advances in both production and consumption? Gasoline, for instance, is one of the few major

Mr. McIvor is a former director and senior vice-president of Exxon Corporation.

commodities, in North America at least, that is as cheap or cheaper than it was 50 years ago (after discounting for inflation).

Second, assuming that they can be made economically competitive, do emerging technologies show promise of being more environmentally-friendly than conventional sources?

A third question is whether society is willing to pay a premium for new, more environmentally-friendly energy sources even if they are not economically-competitive, and even if they are in a form which customers find less attractive than conventional sources.

Perhaps the most illuminating way to get into the subject is to take some time to consider conventional sources: oil, natural gas, coal and electricity. There is no general and overall shortage of economic supplies of any of these. In fact, the opposite is true. While electricity costs are generally regulated, the market-determined prices of oil, gas and coal are at low levels, reflecting their surplus. Oil may present a future problem as the world's surplus-producing capacity becomes even more concentrated in a very few Middle East nations.

For now, the problem is basically political, although this political problem can easily become a major economic one as we know from recent experience. Further, the surplus of these commodities is likely to last for considerable time unless, as noted, oil becomes artificially in short supply for political reasons. Thus, the emerging technologies face a daunting challenge: that of becoming economic when the conventional supplies are relatively cheap.

With that as background, let me go through the roster of emerging technologies and provide an opinion on each. The adjective "emerging" is not entirely fitting for all of the technologies I will discuss since most are hardly new. It would be more appropriate to describe them as potential sources of energy which have not yet become economic enough to be in widespread use, i.e., sources which are at present not economically-competitive with conventional sources. A few of these, if they could be made economic, show promise of being more environmentally-friendly than some conventional sources.

The first ones I will discuss are technologies to provide oil products by un-conventional means. Why do these have any significance when there is a surplus of oil? The reason is that, if they can become economically-competi-tive, they could reduce dependence on the oil supplies that become ever-more concentrated in an area that often presents political problems and they could create wealth in the countries in which they exist.

Enhanced recovery of oil is one such source. Even when primary oil recovery methods are aided by secondary methods such as supplementing natural underground pressure by water injection and other means, usually at least half of the oil in place is left behind as unrecoverable. If countries such as the United States and Canada could recover a significant part of this economically, they would be less dependent on imported oil. The most promising method for tertiary recovery, as this process is known, falls under the name of miscible flooding. In this process a substance such as liquid carbon dioxide which is miscible (i.e., mixable) with the unrecovered oil is injected into the reservoir. It mixes with the oil, increasing its mobility allow-ing it to move more easily from the reservoir to the borehole, and thereby in-creases the amounts ultimately produced.

Miscible flooding has been modestly successful. The factors that constrain it are that the mixing agent is usually very expensive; only reservoirs with certain temperature and pressure regimes are amenable to it; and the process seeks the paths of least resistance in the inevitably heterogeneous reservoirs, just as the primarily- and secondarily-produced oil did, and thus a lot still gets left behind. It is also a slow acting process and cannot be ex-pected to produce sudden bursts of new oil. As with virtually all emerging technologies, much higher oil prices would supply a lot of incentive.

Another somewhat unconventional method of oil production concerns ex-traction of so-called "heavy oil", a substance with which both Canada and Venezuela are extremely well-endowed. These are oils that are so viscous that they flow extremely slowly or not at all into wells that are drilled into the rocks that contain them. Canada, for example, has adopted two means to produce these oils. Where they occur at surface, as at Athabasca, Alberta, the oil-containing rock is mined, the oil separated from the rock fragments, and then upgraded into a high quality crude oil that can be refined into petroleum products. The process is technically successful, and was quite economic while oil prices were high, but it is only marginally economic within the range of prices that have existed since 1986.

The other Canadian method relates to deposits of heavy oil buried 1500 to 2000 feet below the surface, as at Cold Lake, Alberta. There, steam is injected into the reservoir and that reduces the viscosity of the oil so that it will flow into wells. The produced heavy oil is mixed with a diluent that allows pipeline transport to refineries. Again, this process is technically-successful, but only marginally economic at the oil prices of the late-1980s and early-1990s.

It is worth noting that the Cold Lake-type heavy oil production is currently producing from the highest physical quality reservoirs in the area. A significant technological breakthrough and/or higher prices would be necessary if this type of production were to be expanded substantially, because the reservoirs remaining to be developed are of lower physical quality. A very high proportion of Canada's current oil production comes from Athabasca and Cold Lake-type reservoirs, probably in the order of 20 to 25 percent. With conventional light oil production in decline, and discovery prospects generally viewed as very limited, Canada can benefit enormously if heavy oil production could be made more economic through higher prices and/or technological improvements.

Gas conversion is yet another unconventional means by which to produce oil. Natural gas is in long supply around the world, but much of it lies in areas remote from markets and often is not transportable by pipeline, as ocean depths, for example, can pose obstacles between gas deposits and markets. The process takes natural gas (methane) and converts it into a high quality crude oil that can easily be refined into petroleum products. It is a two-stage process that disaggregates the methane and then recombines it with other material to form synthetic crude oil. As with other emerging technologies, the process lies on the wrong side of the economic margin, but not by much. If the capital costs could be reduced, for instance by making it a single-stage, rather than a two-stage process, and if oil prices were somewhat higher, significant amounts of oil could be made from natural gas and transported to market by tanker. Why consider it when crude oil is in long supply? Again, it would create wealth in the nations where the gas exists and would reduce dependence on imports whose security may be fragile. Also, liquid fuels produced in this way from methane could possibly be environmentally superior to those made from crude oil, although this depends on what improvements can be made in conventionally-produced fuels.

I would like now to consider another energy-producing method: nuclear generation of electricity. Again, this is hardly new, the first controlled release of nuclear energy being in 1942. The question is not so much emergence as it is the possibility for re-emergence. It is an economic method, but the problem lies in widespread social resistance to further development. In turn, the social resistance stems from concern for safety, from fear that the products of nuclear plants may be used for the production of nuclear warheads, and from concern for safe disposal of waste products.

The technology for nuclear generation of electricity has been advancing despite the moratorium on new plant construction. One promising development falls under the acronym of IFR which stands for Integral Fast Reactor. The fuel used in this process is in metallic form, with the fuel block encased in a liquid alkali metal such as sodium, which also encases a heat-exchanger and circulating pumps for cooling. The metallic fuel rods encased in liquid sodium have space available for expansion. Loss of cooling results in the metal expanding into the available space and it is thus no longer in a critical state due to loss of density and the reaction either slows down or quits. Also, the reactor waste product can be reprocessed and encased in molten glass which, when solidified, presumably provides a block of safe disposable material. It is my understanding that a lot of work remains before IFR can be shown to be as economic as current processes, but the point is that there may be a technology available that could aid in removing the safety and waste disposal problems that have been of concern with current technology.

Next I would like to consider the subject of motive power -- basically automobiles and other vehicles. I will talk about some means to address the environmental problems currently associated with this area, and about possible replacements for current engines, namely, electric vehicles, which may present less environmental difficulty.

Internal combustion engines have become extremely efficient users of energy, but their use results in exhaust that contains unburned hydrocarbons, carbon monoxide, nitrous oxide, and particulate matter. Large concentrations of vehicles and unfavourable atmospheric conditions, such as exist in the Los Angeles area, present some well-known problems.

In view of the current and projected vehicle population in the United States, it is apparent that a more dramatic lowering of automobile pollution levels within the next 20 years will be achieved more effectively by improving the performance of the internal combustion engine, which uses conventional fuels, than can be expected from any reasonable projection of replacement by electric engines. It is not, however, an either/or situation inasmuch as all the options can be pursued.

Further improvements in the internal combustion engine will likely involve more complete combustion of fuels and greater emission controls. More complete combustion will probably be achieved by tailoring the fuels used, by techniques which control the actual burning process itself, and by keeping lubricants isolated from the combustion. An improvement in exhaust control is likely to come about by means of better control of air-fuel mixtures, which dramatically affect emission, and by clean-up devices. Also, it has been demonstrated recently that a large portion of total emissions takes place in the very short time that it takes an engine and the exhaust catalytic converter to warm up after initial start, and there may be means to prevent this.

With regard to electric vehicles, the newspapers have been keeping up a fairly continuous coverage of their development, and most people by now have attained a fair grasp of the possibilities and problems associated with them. On the plus side, electric cars and trucks in themselves are virtually pollution-free. Of course, their increased use would result in a tremendous surge in the requirement for electric power generation and if this were accomplished by burning fossil fuels other than natural gas, it is questionable whether air pollution would be decreased or just redistributed.

The main problems with electric vehicles stem from the fact that they are powered by conventional batteries. This means that they have a very limited travel range before the batteries need recharging. It also means that they are very expensive and very heavy. According to my recent reading, a small electric car with limited seating capacity (because so much space is taken up by the batteries) retails for considerably more than a conventional luxury car. Thus, it seems that until the range limitation and the cost factors can be dramatically improved, it is unlikely that we will see a significant shift from conventional gasoline and diesel vehicles.

Perhaps the most promising avenue to electric vehicles lies in replacing conventional batteries with fuel cells. A conventional battery wears out and needs recharging because the reactant, usually lead or nickel, becomes completely oxidized as it gives up electrons to produce electricity. On the other hand a fuel cell, as its name implies, has a continuous supply of fuel which can be hydrogen, carbon monoxide, or a hydrocarbon. The supply of fuel to the anode side of the cell and air to the cathode side of the cell results in ionic transport between anode and the cathode together with the emission of electrons and thus electric power. The waste products emitted, along with the electrons, are carbon dioxide, water and heat. While the carbon dioxide may present some problems, no toxic waste is emitted. The promise lies in the fact that fuel cells can be relatively small and light compared to conventional batteries. Also, they do not require recharging. They do need on-board fuel, but this need be no more of a problem than in current internal combustion engines.

So far I have been progressing from the most conventional, established methods of producing energy to the less established and conventional. I am now going to move further in that direction to discuss solar and wind energy, and energy derived from agricultural crops.

I will not spend time talking about solar thermal energy for domestic heating as it has been at the centre of a flurry of experimentation 10 to 30 years ago, on a fairly widespread basis, and it has never caught on. From this I conclude that it is either too inconvenient or too insignificant for now. I will, however, consider solar energy for electric power generation. For those who are unfamiliar with the physics of the matter, when two dissimilar materials in close contact are struck by light, an electric current is generated. Light provides the energy to free electrons to move from one material to the other. In practice, the materials are usually two types of silicon crystals.

So far, this type of electricity generation has been useful in space vehicles where there is no practical alternative; or in very remote areas of the world like Central Australia where small amounts of power are needed for uses such as powering railroad signals. However, for large scale applications such as in major utility electricity generation, it is apparently still not competitive. According to the United States Electric Power Research Institute, which is a major champion of this development, $4 billion dollars of public and private investments in this area up to 1991 has still left its commercial development 10 or so years away. Its attractions are obvious. No pollutants are emitted and the only environmental impact is the land use involved in setting up sunlight collectors, although it would appear that the collectors can cover awesome amounts of land.

Solar energy can also heat water used in conventional electric generation plants so that less conventional fuels such as gas or coal are required to convert it to steam to drive turbines. However, as with direct conversion of sunlight to electricity, this requires a great deal of cost reduction before it will see widespread use.

As a footnote to solar energy, it almost goes without saying that its use, if it becomes economic, will be very uneven due to the very widespread differences in average sunlight hours per year that exist around the globe.

Turning now to wind power, this method shares with solar power the fact that its potential is very unevenly distributed geographically. Wind speeds over 15 miles per hour are generally considered necessary for successful electric power generation, and few areas offer such winds on a reasonably consistent basis. Also, so far only small individual units have been successfully operated relatively maintenance-free over any length of time. Scale-up to larger units has proved difficult. Like solar power, this energy production is free of pollutants, but the land use required can be an environmental or at least an aesthetic problem as anyone who has seen the wind-farms near Palm Springs, California can attest.

The final energy resource I will discuss is motor fuel derived from agricultural crops. Ethanol and methanol are the usual products, and I will discuss ethanol as illustrative. In the United States, this received a considerable spur in the early 1980s from substantial tax-incentives for a 10 percent ethanol (from renewable sources)/90 percent gasoline blend. Considerable capacity was developed but interest waned when the prices of oil dropped in the mid-1980s because pure gasoline became considerably cheaper despite the tax-incentive for ethanol.

Recent interest stems from federal requirements to add oxygenates like ethanol to gasoline. Currently, about seven percent of US gasoline is oxygenated with ethanol. The sole benefit for ethanol use stems from the tax-incentive which is the equivalent to 55 cents per gallon. Thus, ethanol is being propped up by money coming from the more productive parts of the national economy. The drawback is that it has less fuel value than gasoline, so that ethanol blends give lower mileage. It also increases fuel vapour pressure at a time when new fuel regulations call for reduced vapour pressure.

Methanol is similar, but in addition can add toxic material to exhaust and is toxic in itself.

To summarize to this point, only one so-called emerging energy source is economically competitive today with conventional sources, and that is nuclear generated electric power. Its lack of growth in many areas is due to its unacceptability to society for safety and waste disposal reasons, and because its products can be used for nuclear warheads. There is considerable promise of being able to reduce the safety and waste disposal problems.

There are several demonstrated ways to produce oil by unconventional means, and these could help reduce growing dependence on oil from politically fragile areas and also help the economies of countries in which it is produced, including Canada. But each of these particular sources is either uneconomic or only marginally economic at present and would require higher oil prices and/or improved technology to merit greater development.

Conventional fuels currently used in internal combustion engines can likely be made more pollution free by means of improvements to engines and to the fuel itself. Electric vehicles powered by conventional batteries are unlikely to see widespread use any time soon because of travel-range limitations and high cost, and they may simply redistribute pollution rather than prevent it. A more likely avenue to electric vehicles lies in those having power supplied by fuel cells, but this avenue requires significant advance if it is ever to be economic.

Solar electric power and solar heating may become adjuncts to conventional sources of electricity and heat, but it is unlikely that they will achieve widespread use for some time, pending technological and thus economic improvement, and even then the use will be restricted to high sunlight areas.

Wind power is similar inasmuch as it can be utilized only in restricted geographic areas and because even in such areas the problems of scaling up to significant proportions is not yet within reach.

Motor fuels from agricultural products are only in use because of large sub-sidies, and they can be counter-productive in environmental and efficiency terms.

Thus I conclude that conventional fuels (which, by the way, are conven-tional because man is rational and uses the most economic sources of any commodity, including energy) will continue to supply the great bulk of society's energy needs. Further, there are promising ways to make these conventional sources more environmentally-acceptable.

As to Canada's energy future, I would make these suggestions regarding means to make it secure and effective. The first would be to derive the tech-nological means to produce, in an economic manner, its vast quantities of heavy oil, which would of course be made easier by higher oil prices.

The second would be to maintain the technical capability to be able to as-sess, and perhaps to develop and capitalize on, any of the so-called emerg-ing technologies I have described, as these show improvement. How this is best achieved, I leave to your deliberation.

The third is perhaps the most difficult of all. This is the development of a national economy strong enough to import energy of the type that in-digenous sources may be unable to supply. It is well to remember that Japan, for instance, weathered the so-called oil-shocks of the recent past while im-porting virtually all of its hydrocarbon energy because its economy was so strong.

Let me now give some general observations. First I would guess that 50 years from now the world will still rely mainly on oil, gas, coal and electricity for most of its energy. However, the mixture of use will change depending on which forms are made more efficient. Conventional transport fuels can become far more efficient and environmentally-friendly. The same may be true of coal. Natural gas will see greater use. Second, it is well to remember that half of all petroleum use and 100 percent of the growth in use is in developing nations which place a relatively lower priority on environmental concerns. Environmental improvements will take place largely in the current-ly highly developed nations.

I have tried to contribute to this deliberation on Canada's energy future by providing a view of so-called emerging energy sources and their relation to conventional sources. I have purposely attempted to stay away from quantifying the economic hurdles that emerging energy technologies must overcome in order to compete with conventional sources, but I will close with two indices that are representative. To be economic, including a reasonable return on investment, a new well in Saudi Arabia requires oil prices of $3.50 barrel. A new Cold Lake module requires about $26 a barrel. A coal-fired electric plant in the United States needs to sell power for about 6 cents per kilowatt hour to be economic. Solar electricity needs about 25 cents per kilowatt hour.

I hope that I have added something in a knowledge sense, or at least have served to focus your attention on the opportunities and problems involved on the subject.

Forum

Mr. Rob Brandon, AES Canada

I was surprised that Mr. McIvor left out the one emerging technology option that, in my opinion, will likely mean that no new nuclear plants will be built in any country that possesses an adequate natural gas supply. I refer to large gas turbine/combined cycle technology which currently offers life cycle costs at a much smaller plant size than large central utility plants. Perhaps Mr. McIvor could comment on that.

Mr. McIvor

You are right, of course. I did not cover all of the possible energy options. I agree that there is a great deal of promise in combined cycle energy genera- tion. I am not sure that I would necessarily go so far as to say that it would preclude any need for nuclear generation, but certainly your point is valid.

Brigadier-General Michael Webber

Mr. McIvor, I was a little surprised that you did not drag out that hoary old chestnut that has lived in the Sunday supplements for many, many years, that being electricity generation with tidal power. I have seen such a plant in France and I gather that it is economical and it works, but I realize of course

---

This session was chaired by Captain (N) R.H. Thomas, Director of the Centre for National Security Studies at the National Defence College in Kingston.

that it cannot work just anywhere. Do you have any comments on the feasibility of generation by tidal power?

Mr. McIvor

I am sorry but I am really not knowledgeable in that subject. I have heard of the tidal power plant in France, and I know anecdotally that, for example, people have been trying for 75 years or so to capture the tidal power in the Bay of Fundy, but so far without much success.

Another energy option that I did not mention in my talk which I find quite fascinating is the experiment currently going on in Hawaii, not with tides, but one which attempts to exploit the difference between the temperature of sea water 700-800 feet below the surface and the temperature at the surface. Many of you will have read about that experiment which produces power and also desalinates water and includes some irrigation as well. I understand that it is economic but I do not know how much it can be scaled up.

Mr. Nixon

There is a plant in the Bay of Fundy; it has been there for ten years, at Annapolis Royal, and I was there when they were building it as a pilot plant. The problem with tidal power, as with solar and wind power, is that there has to be some way to store it. Energy cannot be stored between the tides, nor can the costs of these types of energy sources be compared with the costs of a base load plant.

Mr. John Zada, CISS Student Intern

Dr. Purdie, I realize that in your lecture this afternoon your regional focus was the Middle East. However, my question concerns the extent to which the South China Sea may prove to be a potential source of oil. Specifically, what nation or nations are in the best positions to capitalize on such, and what would be the overall strategic significance of such a finding?

Dr. Purdie

The South China Sea certainly is one of several areas in the world which are promising ones for oil exploration. China is the location of one of the super giant oil fields of the world; in total there are 37 of these super giants containing over 50 percent of all the oil in the world. Twenty-six of them are in the Middle East.

Mr. McIvor may have something to add.

Mr. McIvor

I do not have a lot to add to that -- I concur entirely with what has been said. The South China Sea remains pretty much to be explored as yet; there has been some exploration in the Gulf of Bo Hai, but I think it is still largely unknown. Certainly it has potential. The sedimentary basin at the Pearl River mouth near Hong Kong has been explored extensively and a couple of small oil fields have been found. It is widely thought that the greatest potential in China is in the basins of the extreme north-west region neighbouring Pakistan, Afghanistan and parts of the former USSR and I believe that China is currently trying to assess the level of interest of Western companies in that particular area.

Mr. Pines

Let me add something to that from the diplomatic or military perspective. In the Spratly Islands there is obviously quite a lot of oil potential. The Spratly Islands are claimed by China, Vietnam, Taiwan, and there is a residual claim as well from the Philippines. The general consensus in the United States Department of State is that the reason for the Chinese arming themselves with aircraft carriers and the like is an intention to seize the Spratly Islands and to intimidate Vietnam. The feeling is that the Vietnamese might well resist that and then there will be an explosion.

Colonel Martin, National Defence College

Mr. McIvor, I found a very interesting paradox in your comments. You have said that people are rational and will use the cheapest energy source available. Since the energy sources from the Middle East are so cheap and there remains a great deal of latitude in which to reduce those prices even further and still make money, what do you think are the prospects for replacing those sources of energy with alternative means?

Mr. McIvor

Another way to pose that question is to ask how successful OPEC, or the reduced OPEC, is going to be over the next few years. In that sense "successful" would be defined as keeping oil prices within a range where, on the low side, they do not damage national revenue aspirations and on the high side they stay below a point where they would do what you just talked about, i.e., start weaning the world off their oil. It is very hard to say. People became very enthused at the end of the last OPEC meeting about six weeks ago, when they thought there was really going to be a system in place, and then, as happens after almost every OPEC meeting within my memory, things started to slide. Yes, they could produce oil much more cheaply than they are doing now. I think they will keep enough cohesion in their cartel so that they will manage somehow or other to keep it in the $17-$18 to $21 per barrel range.

Dr. Eric Solem, National Defence Headquarters

I would like to broaden the discussion slightly and look at what is actually happening inside the oil producing countries. I am wondering how much actual political risk analysis is done by our countries and multinationals. I know of one Canadian company, the Bank of Montreal, that has done a political risk analysis and I would think that there must be more going on. It is not just a question of supply and demand, it is a question of security and of what happens inside these other countries. It would also be necessary to analyze the market, probably taking into account socio-political elements as much as costs.

Mr. McIvor

On behalf of multinationals, since I happen to have worked with one for quite some time, yes, there is an attempt at political forecasting, but I could not claim that it has ever done much good. Of course we all predicted, right down to the time of day, the downfall of the USSR, and we predicted both oil shocks with total precision. We have operations in Chad and we knew that there was going to be an overthrow of the dictatorship every five years -- that was firmly embedded in our brains before we ever went into the country! Of course you know that I am saying that we are just not very good at it. I don't know anybody that is.

Mr. Pines

From the standpoint of governments, (and I used to work for one), we have got people by the score in the US government devoted to that question. They overlap, and when recommendations come to the President, invariably there is one from the energy department, one from the CIA, from the economic people, and one from our people in the State Department, and all of these predict all sorts of different things. In the State Department the standard response to economic questions was "If I knew the answer to that I'd be rich!"

Dr. Purdie

If I could just add a comment to that -- I alluded in my paper to the fact that there have probably been some quite detailed studies conducted in the US on some of these topics, but I am sure also that there are countries of the Middle East looking at them. It must be quite a quandary for them. From the perspective of Saudi Arabia, the UAE and Kuwait, for instance, they have small populations and they do not need a huge revenue, but it probably would be nice to get more money for their oil. But if they increase the price too much then the Western countries are going to go off oil more quickly. Not only that, but their neighbours are going to have more money to buy arms and threaten them. So it is an extremely complex situation.

Mr. McIvor

To indicate how complex it is, we have been asking today what kind of political advice can we seek from the governments of Canada and the US and from multinational companies. We might also ask what economic advice do the oil producing nations have. I think they get some absolutely excellent advice.

Dr. Solem

Just to clarify my earlier point, I was not trying to be critical of multinationals -- I think that to a large extent they were the ones who got us out of the oil crisis in 1974-75, because the government's work was overlapping. I also think, incidentally, that some of the scenario work being done in Exxon is excellent and it shows a much broader way of looking at things than is normally the case.

Mr. McIvor

Well, it has improved. There was a time when it was believed that the objective was forecasting, and fortunately we got over that. The objective is not forecasting. It is to try to embrace the range of possibilities and say "What would I do if I were at that edge of the range, and what would I do if I were at the other end?" so that should the event arrive some of it would actually have been pre-thought. But as to the idea of actually being able to forecast, as I indicated by my earlier comments, most of the people that I worked with said "I give up, it's impossible. However, I can think out what some of the possibilities might be."

Mr. Lawson

Mr. McIvor, there are some who say that mankind is going through a logical development in terms of the energy resources it is using, going through the hydrocarbons and the nasty carbon end of the spectrum and progressing towards the hydrogen end of the spectrum. First, do you ascribe to that logic? What are your views on the hydrogen end?

If I could just add a comment that came to mind when you talked about the use of automobiles -- in looking back on the last century, would someone who lived in the horse and buggy era have predicted that today we would be going into the desert to dig out a sticky deposit and refine it into an explosive liquid, that we would then sit on top of it, pumping it in front of us and exploding it every fraction of a second to take us shopping?

Mr. McIvor

Very cogent point. I can tell you that Exxon would do almost anything to be able to get hydrogen at 10-15 percent less cost than it does today. It could have something to do with new breakthrough-type technologies, but at the moment it is just "grunt and groan" technology. Anyone who could reduce the cost of hydrogen to refineries by 15 percent and get some kind of patent on the process would leave their competitors in the dust.

Your comments are well taken. At first thought it seems half-way preposterous to think of widespread fuelling of things by hydrogen, but as you say, a description of the automotive power that we all take for granted today would have met with the same type of disbelief prior to its invention.

Bob Weaver, Department of National Defence

Mr. McIvor, you mentioned fuel cells in the context of motive power. What about large scale fuel cell stacks for electrical power generation?

Mr. McIvor

I really have to plead that I do not know. The only context in which I have discussed them is in motive power. However, if they can be made success-ful in motive power, I don't see why they could not be made just as success-ful for large scale electrical generation. But that is only an intuitive comment -- I have never in fact pursued that subject.

Mr. Xavier Furtado, CISS Strategic Liaison Officer, Queen's University

Mr. McIvor, given the potential for oil exploration in such areas as the South China Sea and the Middle East, Canadian companies have a great deal of interest there. What sort of role would you see for organizations such as Canadian government trade offices in helping transnational corporations to establish business contracts there? Is that sort of programming useful and if so what could that entail?

Mr. McIvor

My experience has been more recently with what the United States has and has not been able to do. There is not a whole lot that can be accomplished. There is one thing, though. Vietnam was mentioned earlier when we were talking about the Spratly Islands. Over the past few weeks the *Wall Street Journal* has been a running series of articles on Vietnam. In my view at least, the major reason why the United States is not doing business in Vietnam now comes from special interest groups such as MIA (Missing in Action).

The articles are asking whether this is any longer a good reason not to be doing business with Vietnam when Vietnam obviously wants to do business. All kinds of non-US oil companies are already exploring in Vietnam because they don't have any such constraints. So basically, trade organizations would be most helpful in removing any constraints.

George G. Bell

Summation

In his keynote speech, Maurice Strong very clearly indicated that we need strategic planning for the 21st century and, as the turn of the century is less than seven years away, he wondered why we are not beginning the process. He stressed that we are at a crossroad and that we cannot continue on our current path. He then became considerably prescriptive regarding what we can do in Canada in terms of energy efficiency and conservation and in terms of trying to match our national policies to our objectives. Later in his presentation Mr. Strong indicated that we have to look not only at what we are doing in the developed areas of the world, that is the OECD countries, but we must also look at our responsibilities to the underdeveloped areas of the world. He pointed out very clearly that we are dealing with a political-economic dimension which affects both the international and the domestic security policies of our country and those of our allies. He concluded his presentation by stressing the urgency of the situation, cautioning that we have only a very short time -- about two decades -- during which we can "buy time", and after which we must move on.

Following Mr. Strong's address we were presented with the first panel. Ms. Gail Tyerman spoke of Canada and the globalization of energy concerns. She discussed how our participation in international gatherings and international agreements commits us to acting on particular energy issues, and she also discussed the IEA and the challenges it has made to governments. She

Brigadier-General (Retd) George G. Bell, OC, ME, CD, PhD, is the Chairman of the Board of the Canadian Institute of Strategic Studies.

addressed the question of a growing energy demand in the underdeveloped world -- a demand which may be met in part through Canada's export of skills. It must be recognized that, in those regions, it will take more than 20 years to develop the ability to use, and to conserve, energy effectively. In dealing with the subject of our exportation of skills, Ms. Tyerman reminded us that there are areas in the world, such as within the former Soviet empire, where, by gaining access, Canadian business skills might help to restore and improve the situation there. (In fact a later speaker indicated that production in the Soviet Union has gone down rather than up, and agreed that this is one of the areas of real opportunity for Canada.) Ms. Tyerman also pointed out to us that the environmental challenges which were discussed at the Rio summit and at other international conferences are ones that require a mix of measures at the national and international levels and which also require the achievement of consensus in the establishment of common objectives.

Dr. Gerald Angevine presented a very interesting analysis of the world capacities today, detailing the supply levels of energy resources that we have to spend or conserve, and the needs of various parts of the world. Here we began to look at questions that were emphasized later and which focused on the Middle East as a critical area not only for the security of the West but for all the world due to the concentration of oil reserves in that region. But it must be kept in mind that there are other regions, such as those in the developing world, which are in difficult situations that require treatment and therefore a strategic approach to solving the problems in these areas is in our own interests in terms of maintaining world stability.

Mr. Robert Lyman illustrated the changes in policy that have gone on in Canada since the CISS seminar 17 years ago which addressed issues of energy security and the need for an energy strategy for Canada. We seem to have gone through a cycle of change with respect to levels of government involvement in the problem. We have moved back towards privatization but are still confronted with the need for an energy strategy that satisfies our national security needs; one which is comparable and capable of supporting the needs of our economy and the international community.

In his luncheon address Mr. Donald Lawson gave us a very clear demonstration of the capabilities of our nation with regard to the use of nuclear energy. He discussed Canada's future prospects, pointing out our capabilities and our competence. He also indicated that some of the negative public perceptions of nuclear energy are perhaps ill-founded and suggested that there should be a public discussion on the matter of how we solve the problem of re-emerging in the nuclear field as a prime producer.

After lunch, we had the second panel discussion. Mr. Robert Pines, in his presentation, considered the subject of energy security and the free market, and drew attention not only to the integration of our energy industries within Canada, but also to their integration throughout North America, something which will increase as a result of the NAFTA agreement. This of course raises the question of what happens beyond the Western hemisphere -- will there be further integration in the capabilities of Latin America?; do we in fact have the capabilities to deal with the energy deficiencies that exist in the southern regions of the Western hemisphere? Mr. Pines, in his answers to questions, pointed out that there are other areas in the world which are of strategic significance in this regard, such as the Spratly Islands, areas in which countries like China and Vietnam will be contesting for oil resources, because they and other countries in these regions are dependent on oil from the Middle East. We have, therefore, a significant interest in maintaining stability in the Middle East and also in the areas around the South Asian Indo-China peninsula.

I was particularly interested in Dr. John Purdie's presentation because of its focus on the security dimension of energy questions, something which is of strategic importance not only to Canada but to the USA. This is due not only to our vulnerabilities regarding our alternative energy supplies, (remember that we were affected with regard to the Middle East when the regime in Iran changed and we had some problems -- something like six percent of our oil supply was cut off and that resulted in a redistribution of supplies between Canada and the United States which caused considerable discussion of our own energy policies). It also raises broader issues, such as the question of our responsibility regarding the protection of the resources, protection of the transportation systems, and also our need to look at our own capabilities -- our existing capabilities and those that should be developed -- in order to counter the consequences to Canada and to North America should such systems be interrupted.

Mr. William D'Silva in his presentation gave us a very practical and concrete example at the micro-level of what we can do about energy conservation. He discussed what can be done within a particular element of our lives and society in order to further the achievement of the types of efficiencies which Maurice Strong referred to earlier.

Mr. Donald McIvor, who was with us at our energy seminar 17 years ago, was back today to give us a *tour d'horizon* of emerging technologies, their basic importance and their relative potential for near-term and economical development. I was particularly impressed with his treatment of the subject of strategy when he suggested that (1) we need to do something about the drive to maintain and improve the technology of extracting the heavy oil; (2) that we need to maintain, through research and development, the technical capability to capitalize on any or all of these so-called emerging or potential technologies; and (3) that we need to have the national capabilities and national regulations which allow us to import when we are vulnerable in any particular situation.

We have ended up today much where we ended up 17 years ago. We finished the question period at the technological level, seeking solutions to some of the problems of energy use and exploring the questions of what development was necessary in order to achieve those solutions. But we still find ourselves without a national energy strategy, and without a related environmental strategy. We have to recognize that there are political, economic and security dimensions to these strategies and that they are only parts of the framework of the national strategies which Canada still lacks.

For almost 20 years we in the CISS have recognized the need for a matrix of interrelated and interdependent strategies, strategies linking our natural resources, financial and human resources, our knowledge base, our industrial capabilities, and our political system. The urgency is greater today than it was in 1977. I hope that our discussion today will be of some benefit in guiding a strategic approach to the future development of this country and to the overall security dimension, because such an approach is vital to our future progress as a nation.

Documents

Document 1

Energy Implications of NAFTA

On 2 December 1993 the governments of Canada, the United States and Mexico released statements clarifying some aspects of NAFTA which are related to energy.

Throughout the 1993 election campaign Mr. Chretien had maintained that Canada needs to renegotiate NAFTA to obtain "the same energy protection as Mexico". This would entail a review of existing provisions in the Canada-US Free Trade Agreement which require that Canada share energy resources with the US, and which would prevent Canada from charging Americans a higher price for energy than it does Canadians, regardless of possible serious shortages and sharp rises in world oil prices in the future.

As the American refusal to reopen the free trade agreements has remained firm, Prime Minister Chretien's approach took the form of a unilateral declaration to "clarify the limits of Canada's obligations to export energy to the United States".

Text of a statement released by Canada
on 2 December 1993
on Energy and NAFTA

Energy security for Canadians will be an important element in this government's over-all economic priorities.

It will be government policy to promote environmentally responsible and efficient uses of Canadian energy resources and to encourage a robust energy sector.

Canada will continue to be a strong and reliable supplier of energy to its customers, reinforcing its expanding role in North American energy markets.

In the event of shortages or in order to conserve Canada's exhaustible energy resources, the government will interpret and apply the NAFTA in a way which maximizes energy security for Canadians.

The government interprets the NAFTA as not requiring any Canadian to export a given level or proportion of any energy resource to another NAFTA country.

The government will keep Canada's long term energy security under review and will take any measures that it deems necessary to the future energy security of Canadians, including the establishment, if necessary, of strategic reserves, or incentives for oil and gas exploration, development and related activities in order to maintain the reserve base for these energy resources.

Source: Toronto Star, 3 December 1993

Document 2

The Status of Alternative Fuels in Canada

Presentation by Michelle Heath,
Vice-President, Domestic Oil and Transportation, CERI
to the Fourth Annual Alternative Fuels Conference
Austin, Texas, June 1993

I. The Canadian Perspective

The motor fuel industry is very important to Canada. We have a vast land area, 27 million people, 17 million cars, trucks and buses and a very widespread transportation network. Only one percent of these vehicles (198,500 vehicles as of January 1, 1993)[1] are fuelled by alternatives other than gasoline or diesel fuel.

Canada is currently a net oil exporter, but our inexpensive domestic conventional oil supplies are being steadily depleted. In fact, we currently import over half a million barrels of light/medium oil a day to meet the feedstock requirements of our refiners. This heavy reliance on crude oil to meet the energy demands of the transportation sector can, therefore, have wide ranging effects on our economy.

Historically, the objectives of Canadian energy policy have been the development of Canadian resources and the provision of reasonably priced energy to all regions of our economy. Though Canada remained a net exporter of crude oil after the oil price shocks of the 1970s, the federal government became concerned about our long-term crude oil supply and concluded that the use of alternative fuels could help to ensure energy self-sufficiency as well as promote the use of other domestic energy resources. Thus, the federal government initiated the alternative fuels program in 1980.

Current policy objectives are much the same but the focus has shifted somewhat. Diversity and regional development have become increasingly important issues in these difficult economic times. Nationally, however, it is environmental considerations and the effects of transportation fuels on the atmosphere, both locally and globally, which are the major concerns promoting renewed interest in clean burning alternative energy sources.

The alternative fuels currently being tested and/or used in Canada include natural gas, propane, methanol, ethanol, the reformulates, hydrogen and electric propulsion. Fuel quality, availability and price/economics, distribution and refuelling infrastructure, as well as user requirements are issues being examined for each of these fuels. This paper will discuss the current use of natural gas, propane, methanol and ethanol in the Canadian transportation industry as well as briefly examine the environmental implications and economic potential of these fuels in relation to gasoline and diesel fuel.

II. Natural Gas for Vehicles (NGV)

Natural gas is one of Canada's most abundant fuel resources. With over 100 TCF of proven natural gas reserves in Canada and a very large potential reserve base from both conventional and unconventional sources, it is understandable why Canada's policy makers are promoting interest in natural gas fuel development.

In line with its energy policy, the federal government provides strong support to the development of an NGV market in Canada. Currently, in markets served by Alberta gas, the Federal government offers a $500 conversion incentive per vehicle along with a $1,000 incentive for installing a vehicle refuelling appliance (VRA). Under the Natural Gas Fuelling Station Program, the government contributes $50,000 towards the cost of each public fuelling station. To offset the high costs of installing on-site NGV refuelling facilities and encourage private station development, the Commercial Compression Program contributes 25 percent of the capital costs of commercial NGV compressors, up to a maximum of $50,000 per compressor. Additionally, natural gas as a vehicle fuel is exempt from Federal Excise Taxes, although it is subject to the Goods and Services Tax (GST).

The Federal government incentive program has been in existence for several years and is approved to March 31, 1994. It is financed from the Market Development Incentive Payments Fund (MDIP) which is a fund arising out of an agreement between the Federal and Alberta governments to build markets for Alberta gas. This program does not extend into British Columbia which is detrimental to the successful development of an NGV program in that province.

There are other more generic federal incentive programs which affect the use of this fuel as well, in addition to a variety of provincial and utility incentive programs. NGV is exempt from road taxes in five provinces. Ontario refunds the provincial sales tax of eight percent to a maximum of $1,000 for vehicles converted to natural gas within 180 days of being purchased. The $1,000 ceiling does not apply to transit and school buses however, which means a bus costing $50,000 would earn a $4,000 refund, almost the cost of conversion.[2]

These programs are further strengthened by the complementary conversion incentives offered by a number of distribution utilities. Cylinder rental programs reduce the initial capital outlay at the time of conversion and allow the utilities control over the cylinder inspection and recertification program. Utilities have also supported the development of conversion shops and fuelling stations.

Government incentive programs are currently necessary catalysts for the development of NGV in Canada for two reasons... to ensure the viability of converting and as evidence of government endorsement of the benefits of this industry to Canadians. Over the past decade in Canada, 34,000 vehicles have been converted to dual fuel NGV/gasoline operation.[3] Approximately 38 percent of the converted NG vehicles are located in British Columbia, 41 percent in Ontario, 15 percent in Quebec and only five percent in Alberta, Canada's largest gas producing province. Fifty-nine percent of these conversions are utilized as commercial vehicles.[4]

Natural gas has also been recognized as an attractive alternative fuel in transit applications because of the high fuel consumption, regularity of routes, the ability to fuel and service the fleet in one location, and the need for cleaner buses in our downtown areas. In Canada there are 80 buses operating on natural gas in Toronto, Hamilton, Mississauga, and Vancouver. Seventy-five of these buses were manufactured by Ontario Bus Industries and are equipped with Cummins L-10 spark-ignited natural gas engines. The Vancouver buses are designed for dual-fuel technology using Detroit Diesel 6V92 engines.

In addition to 72 private fuelling stations in service, 120 retail stations have been opened. As well, industry has installed more than 1,100 vehicle refuelling appliances (VRAs) in test sites for both residential and commercial applications. Around 64 million litres of conventional fuels were displaced in 1992 by 60 million cubic metres of natural gas used for fuelling vehicles.

III. The Environment and Gaseous Fuels

Canadian consumers, along with the legislators of Canada's energy policies, are becoming increasingly aware of the need to consider the global concern for environmental pollution. A number of the environmental issues are directly affected by the burning of fossil fuels including the greenhouse phenomena, the ground-level formation of ozone, carbon monoxide, and the carcinogenic effects of aromatics and aldehydes.

Regarding the greenhouse phenomena, emissions testing to date indicates alternative transportation fuels produced from fossil fuel feedstocks such as coal, natural gas, and crude oil will not result in a significant reduction in greenhouse gas emissions, whereas improvements in vehicle efficiency and renewable biomass resources, depending on how they are processed and used and whether they are replenished, may.

Both natural gas and propane are capable of producing less tailpipe CO_2 emissions than either gasoline or diesel fuel vehicles. The reason for this is that they contain less carbon per unit of energy than either gasoline or diesel fuel, and are more efficient than gasoline therefore providing greater travel distances per unit of energy.

Natural gas and propane burn more efficiently than gasoline, as they enter the engine cylinders already vaporized. The result is generally fewer exhaust emissions; carbon monoxide levels are much lower, and hydrocarbons are generally lower as well. However, as both these fuels burn at higher temperatures than gasoline, nitrogen oxide emissions, which are temperature dependent, tend to increase. Nitrogen oxide emissions can, however, be further controlled by means of exhaust gas recirculation.

It is important to note that, when buying a conversion kit for either propane or natural gas, it must be properly installed by a mechanic certified to convert gasoline vehicles into dual-fuel vehicles or else emissions may increase when operating the vehicle on gasoline and may be the same as for gasoline or insignificantly lower when operating on the gaseous fuel. Dedicated natural gas or propane vehicles would likely achieve much better emissions standards than dual-fuel (gasoline or diesel/natural gas or propane) vehicles.

The particulates being emitted into the atmosphere are major contributors to smog formation. With proper fuel metering, diesel engines converted to dual-fuel will provide a reduction in particulate emissions when compared to conventional diesel operations. However, should the fuel control system for natural gas and diesel fuel be improperly adjusted, over-fuelling can result in smoke.

IV. Propane

Propane is the most widely used alternative to gasoline and diesel fuel in Canada, with over three million litres per day being consumed as a transport fuel. Approximately 80 percent of Canada's propane, over 20 million litres per day, are produced at gas plants in Western Canada as a byproduct of natural gas production. Of the nearly 160 barrels of propane produced daily in Canada, 30 percent is used for heating, 12 percent for transport, 7.8 percent for the petrochemical industry and 4.7 percent for enhanced oil recovery. This leaves 45.5 percent of Canada's production available for export or increased use in our domestic markets.

A comprehensive propane infrastructure is in place, including processing, pipelines, import terminals, underground storage and filling stations. Propane is currently being sold in Canada at over 5,000 outlets and the 170,000 propane vehicles in operation currently consume around 1.3 billion litres of propane per year.

The federal government's propane program was initiated in 1981. The government offered conversion grants of $400 to help reduce the $1,200-$1,400 cost of converting a commercial vehicle to operate on propane. The aim was to encourage commercial market development to a level whereby propane sales would account for one or two percent of the motor fuel market, a level felt to be self-sustainable. In 1984, the government expanded its conversion grant program to include dual-fuelled and non-commercial vehicles. The federal government's propane vehicle conversion target was met in 1985 and the conversion grants were eliminated.

Ensuring further market growth of propane in the Canadian transportation industry will require evolving vehicle engine technologies, including throttle body vapour injection and multi-port vapour and liquid injection; more convenient refuelling features will also be necessary.

To facilitate the necessary research and development, the industry has set up the Canadian Auto Propane Council (CAPC). Some of the initiatives which CAPC is involved with include: a project with IMPCO Technologies of Cerritos, California to design an Alternate Fuel Electronics fuel system; a project with ORTECH International of Mississauga, Ontario focusing on researching propane fuel injection and the development of a gaseous fuel injection system; and an agreement with Chrysler Canada to build a concept original equipment manufactured alternative fuelled vehicle as a first step to producing propane powered vehicles.

One of the major drawbacks to the expansion of the propane industry has been in persuading the original equipment manufacturers (OEMs) to produce propane cars, trucks and buses and assure updated propane carburation and fuel systems. That obstacle is in the process of being remedied with the production of three- and five-ton propane trucks by Ford Motor Company which will be available to consumers this year. Also, Chrysler Canada Ltd. will have propane-powered pickup trucks and vans produced and ready for sale in the market by 1995.

V. The Environment and Alcohol Fuels

In comparison with gasoline, the exhaust emissions from vehicles burning ethanol or methanol contain negligible amounts of aromatics, reduced hydrocarbons (HC) and carbon monoxide (CO) levels but increased nitrogen oxide (NO_x) emissions. Another advantage of alcohol fuels is that their combustion in diesel engines results in very low particulate emissions. However, the aldehyde fraction of unburned alcohol fuels is appreciably greater than for hydrocarbon-based fuels; therefore, catalytic converters are needed to reduce these emissions at the tailpipe.

VI. Methanol

Canada is one of the largest methanol producing nations in the world. Eighty-five percent of the two million tonnes produced (enough to fuel about a half-million vehicles) is being exported to the United States, Japan and Europe. However, methanol for vehicle use in Canada is still in the development stage; volumes are small, distribution costs high. There are presently 45 methanol cars in Canada and one public fuelling station in Scarborough, Ontario. As well, we have 16 methanol buses. With both the provincial and federal governments currently granting tax breaks to alternative fuels, methanol can compete with regular gasoline on a cost per litre basis. At the Scarborough facility M-85 sells for 32 cents per litre (cpl) when gasoline is priced at 55 cpl.

Methanol is also being used as a feedstock for methyl tertiary butyl ether (MTBE), an oxygenate which, when added to gasoline, results in a cleaner burning fuel that can be formulated to reduce emissions of carbon monoxide and ground level ozone. Currently Alberta Envirofuels Inc. (owned equally by Chevron Canada Limited and Neste Canada Inc.) has an MTBE plant in Edmonton, Alberta with a capacity of 530,000 tonnes per year, most of which is being exported to the United States.

As with the gases, there are a number of challenges facing the introduction of methanol as a fuel and as a feedstock for MTBE. These include the development of a public fuelling infrastructure, continued research in the areas of flame visibility, and the environmental effects of MTBE, particularly in cold climates.

VII. Ethanol

Ethanol, produced from biomass, is another renewable energy source with potential for use as an alternative fuel. Current technology suggests that the feedstock requirements of an ethanol industry may provide markets for Canadian grains which are difficult to sell in the domestic and world marketplace. Presently there are around 22 million litres of ethanol being produced from biomass for fuel in Canada. The ethanol is being marketed in low level blends in five provinces.

Research and development activities continue to focus on improving the ethanol process technology (particularly ethanol from cellulose or woody feedstocks) to reduce the costs of production. It was recently noted in *Bio-Joule* magazine that it is possible to produce ethanol for around $0.45 to $0.51 per litre. Although steam explosion pretreatment, fermentation and ethanol recovery are considered mature technologies with little possibility for advancement, both enzyme production and hydrolysis are areas where improvements can occur. Feedstock costs could also be reduced.

VIII. The Economics of Natural Gas, Propane, Methanol and Ethanol in Relation to Gasoline and Diesel Fuel

Since gasoline and diesel prices fluctuate with crude oil prices, the comparative economic analysis is directed at determining the per litre equivalent price differential necessary for each of the alternative fuels examined to maintain a competitive pricing position in the current market-place.

The financial analysis indicates that for the individual conversions of smaller light/medium size vehicles outside of fleets, NGV economics are very marginal. Assuming a five-year life, personal automobiles travelling up to 20,000 kilometres per year would incur losses if the vehicle conversion costs were as high as $2,800 and compressor costs of $1,500 were included. On the other hand, where dedicated natural gas vehicles become available from the OEMs and the incremental cost to the consumer is simply the differential cost between the natural gas cylinders being utilized and the gasoline tank which they replace, even the personal-use vehicles become financially viable. Further, high mileage natural gas fleets can accrue substantial savings with differentials as low as five cents per litre equivalent (15.8 cents per gallon (US/US)) required to recover incremental costs associated with conversion and the refuelling infrastructure. The 1992 national average litre equivalent price differentials between natural gas and regular unleaded gas and diesel fuel were 26 and 21 cents (81 and 66 cents per gallon (US/US)) respectively.

Propane is also competitively viable when considered as a fuel for high mileage fleet vehicles. However, as with natural gas vehicles, the vehicles currently being converted to operate on propane are retrofits (not factory produced models) and therefore the costs incurred, although not as high as for natural gas, are difficult to recover over the life of a personal-use vehicle. Propane, unlike natural gas, is not constrained in Canada by the need for development of a national refuelling infrastructure. Even when fleets maintain their own propane refuelling facilities, the capital costs incurred are about one-fifth those necessary for compressed natural gas.

Propane's market niche lies with light/medium commercial vehicles (i.e. taxi-cab companies and delivery services). These vehicles can be converted at a relatively inexpensive cost, and their high annual mileage and resulting use of large volumes of fuel provide for the possibility of relatively short payout periods and substantial long-term fuel savings as price differentials as low as 4 cents per litre equivalent (12.6 cents per gallon (US/US)) are required to recover conversion costs assuming the current refuelling infrastructure is adequate. Though provincial propane prices vary, the 1992 national average price differentials between propane and regular unleaded gasoline and diesel fuel were 20 and 15 cents per litre (63 and 47 cents per gallon (US/US)) respectively.

One constraining factor to the transportation market demand for propane relates to the fact that propane is an internationally traded commodity in direct competition with gasoline and #2 fuel oil. An aberration in the normal weather pattern can, therefore, result in the increased demand for propane in the heating market and a short-term strain on supplies available for the transportation market plus increases in the posted and spot prices.

The financial analysis for methanol indicates that methanol also has the potential to compete in the transportation fuel market. Methanol vehicle costs, with large volume demand, are less than the present costs of converting to propane or natural gas. In part, this reflects the interest of the original equipment manufacturers and the manufacture of flexible fuel and/or dedicated alcohol vehicles in response to contracts in various parts of North America and Brazil. A price differential as low as nine cents per litre (28.4 cents per gallon US/US)), which is achievable at prevailing methanol production costs, can make dedicated methanol or flexible fuel vehicles viable with optimum alcohol use. As with the other alternatives, however, when the costs of the refuelling stations are incorporated into the analysis, the size of the fleet of vehicles being converted becomes a key variable in determining the overall cost to the individual consumer or fleet manager.

Even with the existing federal and various provincial incentives, current economics of ethanol production make neat or near-neat fuel ethanol nonviable. On the other hand, as an oxygenate with a high octane rating that provides a market for Canadian grains, it remains a candidate for increased growth in the transportation market.

IX. Conclusions and the Future of NGVs in Canada

The alternative fuels market in Canada is still evolving and continues to face many challenges, the most difficult being that of competing against gasoline and diesel fuel. But both the emissions testing to date and the economics performed suggest that there are niche markets which would prove viable for each of the alternative fuels discussed. From the consumer's perspective, however, the alternatives of choice will have to be as good as, or better than, gasoline and/or diesel fuel.

Natural gas is the lowest priced alternative fuel in Canada. Greater use in our automobiles offers the potential for increased security of supply and a cleaner environment. Seventy-five percent of the vehicles in Canada operate in areas already serviced by a natural gas distribution network. And yet there are barriers to the commercialization of NGVs which must be overcome. Conversion costs, currently in excess of $3,000, must be reduced to levels affordable to the consumer.The refuelling infrastructure must be expanded if the public is to be persuaded to convert to natural gas or the OEMs to produced dedicated NG vehicles. Most importantly, the Canadian public awareness of the benefits of natural gas as a clean, safe, non-toxic and plentiful supply source must be increased.

Notes

1. Propane Gas Association of Canada Inc., A Presentation to the BC Alternative Fuels Task Force, Calgary, Alberta, February 1993.

2. Canadian Gas Association, Presentation to the Alternative Fuels Task Force, Mississauga, Ontario, March 1993.

3. Ibid.

4. Schingh, Marie. An Overview of the Canadian Federal Alternative Fuels Program. Continental Conference of Alternative Fuels, September, 1992, Oklahoma City.

Document 3

Nuclear Energy: A New, Safer Way?

Barry James
(Reprinted from the International Herald Tribune
November 27-28, 1993)

A leading theoretical physicist has proposed the use of particle accelerators to produce nuclear energy with minimal radioactive waste and only a small residue of plutonium.

The stockpiling of plutonium is seen as a threat to the world's stability, because not only is it the main component in nuclear weapons but it is also one of the most toxic substances known to man.

In his last coup before leaving the director-general's seat at CERN, the European Laboratory for Particle Physics in Geneva, at the end of the year, Carlo Rubbia said his proposed "energy amplifier" would overcome safety concerns about present reactors.

Experts at the International Atomic Energy Agency in Vienna said the idea could work in theory but that the cost of developing the technique might be prohibitively expensive. Their attitude is one of a cautious wait and see, a spokesman said.

At a scientific seminar at CERN this week, Mr. Rubbia suggested that thorium, a plentiful element, could be used as fuel if bombarded with a beam of neutrons produced in a particle accelerator.

Thorium on its own produces insufficient neutrons to create a self-sustaining nuclear reaction. Mr. Rubbia said the addition of neutrons from an accelerator would turn thorium into uranium-233, which can sustain a nuclear reaction. Scientists believe there is more potential energy in thorium than in hydrocarbon fuels and uranium combined.

Mr. Rubbia said the process could not become critical, or out of control, because the reaction would stop the instant the neutron beam was switched off.

Accelerators are tunnels in which magnets and enormous inputs of power are used to collide subatomic particles at almost the speed of light to discover the origins of matter and energy.

In this way, Mr. Rubbia and a fellow physicist discovered the W and Z particles that carry the so-called weak force involved on radioactive decay. They received the 1984 Nobel Physics Prize for the discovery.

Mr. Rubbia said computer studies indicated that one ton of thorium would produce only 200 grams of plutonium, one-fifth as much as a conventional uranium reactor. According to the Stockholm International Peace Research Institute, up to 190 tons of weapons-grade plutonium will result from the reprocessing of fuel from conventional power-reactors in the 1990s.

Mr. Rubbia said his proposed process would produce fission fragments rather than highly radioactive waste requiring thousands or millions of years to decay. He said the fragments would decay to the radioactive level of natural uranium within about 300 years, which he called "an acceptable delay for institutional storage."

Mr. Rubbia, who explained his process to French nuclear physicists in Paris on Friday, has created a complete computer simulation of his suggested process. He also put the idea before the experiments committee at CERN, which will decide whether accelerator experiments should go ahead.

"I don't imagine any impediments will be placed in his way," a colleague said.

The accelerator experiments would provide a basis for deciding whether the process merits further investment.

Energy experts said that given the present financial climate it would be difficult to launch an untried new energy system. They said the relatively low price of oil, gas and coal would discourage heavy investment in the process.

But Mr. Rubbia said the demand for nuclear power - which supplies about 6.5 percent of the world's energy needs - would take off in the future because of environmental concerns about burning fossil fuels and increased demand for energy from developing countries. He also said his system could build on existing technologies.

In his paper, Mr. Rubbia acknowledges work taking place at the Los Alamos National Laboratory, where scientists have proposed using particle beams to absorb the neutrons in high-level radioactive waste. This could shorten the amount of time required for radioactivity to decline to safe levels.

Document 4

The Economic Effects of the Canadian Nuclear Industry

Summary of a report from Ernst & Young
Sponsored by Atomic Energy of Canada Limited
October 1993

A. Study Objectives

The objective of Ernst & Young with this study was to document the economic contribution of the nuclear industry in Canada and abroad to the Canadian economy. Therefore, the major costs and benefits associated with government investment, largely federal, in the nuclear industry were documented.

In more immediate terms, another goal was to update the previous study of the effects of the Canadian nuclear industry completed by Leonard and Partners Limited in 1978.

B. Study Scope

The term "nuclear industry" was defined to include all activities directly related to the design, construction, equipment supply and operation of nuclear power facilities. This covered activities such as research and development, engineering, manufacturing, uranium mining and refining and maintenance services.

For the purposes of this study, the scope did not include activities in spin-off industries such as health sciences or agriculture that rely on nuclear technology. The only exceptions to this were Nordion International Inc. and Theratronics International Ltd., both of which were divisions of Atomic Energy of Canada Limited (AECL) until 1989. Beyond a qualitative discussion, our definition of economic effects also did not attempt to financially quantify the environmental and medical benefits from the use of nuclear technology.

We defined "government investment" as federal government expenditures on the nuclear industry including appropriations and write-offs. We recognize that this federal investment is incremental and has been leveraged by other public and private sector investments which together have resulted in the effects described in this study.

With respect to effects, both economic and non-economic effects in aggregate form, i.e., for the nation as a whole, were sought. Impacts on specific regions/communities are presented only where such information/analysis was readily available.

C. Study Methodology

The information required to conduct this impact study was collected using the following five methods.

- Mail survey of the 154 Canadian companies which supply products and/or services to the nuclear industry (a response rate of 50% was achieved),
- Interviews with 35 industry stakeholders,
- Review of 150 relevant reports and documents,
- Case studies of 5 successful companies, and
- Input-output analysis using Statistics Canada's Open Output Determination Model.

The methodology was designed to obtain the most up-to-date and reliable data directly from the primary sources. Where it was necessary to use secondary data, we have cross-checked/verified them with the primary sources to the extent possible. All sources, whether primary or secondary, have been referenced accordingly in the report. Limitations with the data have also been identified where relevant.

D. Major Findings

The major findings of our study are quantified where possible and, in our view, represent conservative, minimum estimates of effects.

Energy Supply

1. The Canadian nuclear industry plays a significant role in the provision of energy in Canada.

– Between 1962 and 1992, nuclear energy production in Canada rose from 22 GWh to 76,022 GWh (GW = Gigawatt = 10^9 watt).

– In 1992, nuclear energy supplied 15% of Canada's electricity requirements. Forty-eight percent of Ontario's electricity needs, 30% of New Brunswick's and 3% of Quebec's were met by nuclear energy last year.

– The industry produced electricity valued at $3.7 billion in 1992.

– With the completion of the Darlington station in 1993, nuclear energy provides almost 20% of Canada's electricity.

Economic Effects

2. In developing Canada's nuclear energy capability, the federal government has appropriated a net amount of $4.7 billion to AECL since 1952 in as-spent dollars. The economic effects of these appropriations are as follows:

– *Overall Impact on GDP*

   Using Statistics Canada's Open Output Determination Model, we conservatively estimate that the total contribution of the nuclear industry to Canada's Gross Domestic Product (GDP) from 1962 to 1992 was at least $23 billion.[1] In simple terms, over 90% of the industry inputs required to generate electricity from nuclear power (valued at $3.7 billion in 1992) are sourced in Canada. This means that imports constitute less that 10% of the inputs and Canadian products and services constitute over 90% of the inputs.

   The GDP contribution was calculated using the value from the nuclear generation of electricity and the Canadian content of all CANDU reactors sold abroad. It does not reflect nuclear research and development activities. If these were included, the impact of the nuclear industry on Canada's GDP would be even greater.

– *Direct Employment*

   We estimate direct employment in the nuclear industry in 1992 at about 30,000 jobs. Survey results suggest that approximately 90% of these jobs are full-time. Part-time employees work an average of 35-40% of their time on nuclear-related activities.

Between 1989 and 1992, direct employment increased by approximately 9%. The distribution of direct employment in 1992 by area of activity is estimated as follows:

Ontario Hydro	12,000[2]
Hydro-Quebec	650
New Brunswick Power Corp.	450
AECL	4,500
Private sector suppliers	8,500
Uranium	2,200
Public sector administration	350
Construction at Darlington	870
Other	350
TOTAL JOBS (approx)	**30,000**

Construction, refurbishing and/or maintenance activities associated with CANDU reactors are reflected in the private sector suppliers' employment numbers.

- *Indirect Employment*

In addition to direct employment, the nuclear industry also helps support other jobs in the Canadian economy. More specifically, we conservatively estimate that a minimum of 10,000 jobs in other sectors indirectly depend on the nuclear industry. This level of indirect employment is sustained even when there are no reactors under construction at home or overseas.

Based on analysis of the recently signed Wolsong 3 and 4 contracts, Industry and Science Canada (ISC) estimates the domestic employment multiplier to be 2.5 for the construction phase of a new export reactor project. This means that indirect employment in Canada will rise by 2,500 when each new CANDU export project is being built abroad.

Induced employment was not calculated. Induced employment is that which is created through the spending of disposable income. However, jobs in the Canadian economy do depend on the purchases made by the employees of the nuclear industry when they spend their pay cheques.

– *Sales*

In 1993, Canada holds 7% of the world's market share of nuclear reactors and 10% of the market share of the nuclear reactors under construction. A twin reactor order from South Korea, valued at over $1.0 billion was Canada's single largest export order in 1992.

Based on our survey analysis, we estimate that private sector companies who supply nuclear products and services have generated total sales of $9.4 billion between 1988 and 1992. Compared to sales of $350 million in 1977, this represents a compounded growth of 23% annually. In real terms, it represents approximately a 17% compounded annual growth rate.

At present, the split between domestic and export sales from private sector suppliers is 60%/40%. In the future, the industry expects this split to reverse. More specifically, exports are to account for 60% of total sales by 1998.

In addition to these private sector sales, AECL generated revenues of approximately $1.3 billion in five years between 1988 and 1992 and $335 million in 1992. The breakdown of these revenues is as follows:

| Commercial nuclear operations | = $808 million (1988-1992)
= $209 million (1992) |
| Cost sharing and commercial
R & D activities | = $484 million (1988-1992)
= $126 million (1992) |

– *Tax Revenues*

Our study estimates that the federal government receives approximately $700 million in tax revenues annually from the nuclear industry in the form of income and sales taxes. This figure excludes corporate income taxes.

– *Exports*

Annual exports of nuclear products and services in 1991 were approximately $550 million. This comprised:

| Uranium exports | = $290 million |
| AECL exports | = $100 million |

Other exports (i.e. Theratronics) = $100 million

Nuclear electricity exports   = $61 million
by the utilities

With respect to CANDU project sales, the confirmed sale of two additional CANDU 6 reactors to South Korea is expected to result in more than $1.5 billion in new business in Canada during the construction lifetime of the entire 4-unit Wolsong (1976 to 1999). Ninety percent of the products and services for these exports to South Korea will be sourced in Canada (excluding construction).

– *Positive Trade Balance*

Canada's nuclear industry has a positive trade balance given its significant exports and limited imports. Specifically, the nuclear industry imports approximately $50 million worth of specialized equipment each year and special metals and alloys like zirconium for use as fuel bundle cladding or sheathing materials

Estimates of the size of the positive trade balance vary. Using the figures referred to above and subtracting imports of approximately $50 million, our study estimates that the nuclear industry in 1991 generated a positive trade balance of $500 million.

Based on its definition of the high technology components of the nuclear industry, Industry and Science Canada estimated that the nuclear industry generated a trade surplus of $250 million in 1991. In fact, by ISC calculation, nuclear and aerospace were the only two Canadian industries in the high technology area with surplus trade balances. All other high technology areas including telecommunication and biotechnology had trade deficits.

Industry	$ millions
Aerospace	$950
Nuclear	**$250**
Biotechnology	($60)
Opto-electronics	($190)
Weapons	($280)
Material Design	($500)

Industry	$ millions
Computers and Telecommunications	($3800)
Computer Integrated Manufacturing	($1300)
Electronics	($1500)
Life Sciences	($1900)

Source: Industry and Science Canada, 1992

However, among the exports defined as high-tech is natural uranium oxide, which has the lion's share (98%) of the nuclear positive trade balance. The remainder consists of nuclear reactors, or parts of, and instrumentation, fuel elements and other special uranium compounds.

– *Foreign Exchange Savings or Positive Contribution to the Current Account Deficit*

Ontario Hydro estimates that, from 1965 to 1989, nuclear energy has saved the Canadian economy approximately $17 billion (1989 dollars) in foreign exchange. In the absence of nuclear energy, this money would have been spent on importing coal from the United States to Ontario and importing oil or coal into Quebec and the Atlantic provinces. Ontario Hydro estimates that, in the 1990s, foreign exchange savings will amount to approximately $1 billion a year.

– *Regional Development*

The nuclear industry is dynamic and opportunities for private companies emerge in cycles depending on whether new CANDU reactors are being constructed. For this reason, the number of companies vary from year to year. In 1992, we estimate that there were 154 Canadian companies that supplied manufactured or engineered products and/or services to AECL and the electric power generating utilities.

Fifty-eight percent of the companies we identified are based in Ontario, 14% in Alberta and 12% in Quebec. Companies located in Alberta are mainly small suppliers who provide products and services to the uranium industry. The remaining provinces have 16% of the private-sector suppliers. Sixty-six percent of these companies are in manufacturing, 30% in engineering and design, and 16% in R&D.

Survey results reveal that one quarter of these companies are new entrants to the nuclear industry, i.e., they started supplying nuclear products and services in the last ten years. In terms of percentage growth, New Brunswick has seen a doubling of suppliers since 1978 (albeit from a small base), Quebec has seen a 22% growth, Ontario has seen an 18% growth, and Alberta has seen a 14% growth.

Spin-Off Benefits

In addition to the economic benefits identified above, the nuclear industry has realized several "spin-off" benefits that have created new industries and domestic and export markets for Canada in the following three major areas: medical sciences, environment and agriculture.

For example, Theratronics (formerly the Medical Products Division of AECL) has built over 1,300 of the world's cobalt therapy machines. Every year, an estimated one-half million people are treated for cancer, in 70 countries, using these machines.

Nordion, also a former division of AECL, is the world's leading supplier of Cobalt-60 irradiation facilities used in the sterilization of medical and surgical equipment. Nordion supplies and markets most of the radioisotopes used in medical diagnosis. About 7 million people benefit from these isotopes every year.

Irradiation is also used to sterilize insects, to improve the nutritional characteristics of feed livestock and to gauge optimal hormone levels and breeding times. The combined result is more productive and disease-resistant livestock.

In terms of environmental benefits, nuclear energy is a clean form of energy, particularly in comparison to fossil sources such as coal and oil. Because there is no combustion during the nuclear reaction, nuclear energy does not emit acid gases or carbon dioxide (CO_2). This helps avert acid rain and reduces global warming (the "greenhouse effect").

In addition, the demanding quality assurance processes developed in and for the nuclear industry have had a very broad and beneficial impact in many sectors.

Enhanced Competitiveness

According to the Canadian companies surveyed, participation in the nuclear industry has helped enhance their competitiveness in the following ways.

- it has helped improve the quality of products and services for 33% of supplier companies surveyed,
- it has facilitated increased access to foreign nuclear markets for 22%,
- it has facilitated increased access to new markets in non-nuclear areas for 20% of companies, and
- it has improved the safety standards of 12% of the companies surveyed.

Summary of Benefits

In summary, government appropriations for AECL were $167 million in 1992. This investment levered other public and private sector investments which together resulted un the following economic effects:

- Produced energy valued at $3.7 billion in 1992
- Directly employed 30,000 people in 1992
- Created indirect employment of at least 10,000 in 1992
- Generated federal tax revenues of $700 million in 1992
- Generated nuclear trade surplus of $500 million in 1991
- Generated revenues of $335 million for AECL from commercial nuclear operations and R&D activities in 1992
- Resulted in foreign exchange savings of approximately $1 billion in 1992

Conclusions

We conclude that the economic effects of the Canadian nuclear industry have been substantial. Over the past 31 years, the GDP contributions of the nuclear power generation industry has been at least $23 billion (as-spent dollars). The GDP contributions for 1992 were $3.5 billion.

The nuclear industry also supports at least 40,000 direct and indirect Canadian jobs associated with both nuclear research and CANDU technology.

Spin-off benefits from the nuclear industry have augmented Canadian technological and commercial capabilities in other sectors such as agriculture, medicine and the environment. For example, commercial operations such as Theratronics are directly linked to the government's decision to appropriate funds for the development of nuclear applications.

Increases quality standards for Canadian manufacturing companies are a result of the stringent standard demanded for goods produced for nuclear application. Such standards have allowed companies supplying the industry to gain a competitive advantage in technical design and engineering.

Until recently, AECL had focused primarily on enhancing the capacity of the domestic market. At the present, nuclear power is supplying close to 20% of Canada's electricity needs. However, there are no concrete plans for developing new nuclear generating plants in Canada and, with the temporary decline for new domestic nuclear capacity, the industry is pursuing export opportunities. This strategy has been successful as seen by the recent signing of the Wolsong 3 and 4 contracts with South Korea.

Based on our study, we conclude that the Canadian nuclear industry has the capability to sustain current levels of economic activity through export projects assuming the current base of 22 nuclear reactors in Canada is maintained. Our findings indicate that there is an excess of electricity on the national market is present. However, assuming that this situation will transform into a long term trend is ill-advised. Long term predictions show electricity needs will increase as the Canadian economy either stabilizes or grows. Since nuclear is an important component in Canada's electricity mix, substitution by an alternative fuel type would be costly in both economic and environmental terms.

In 1992, the nuclear industry had a positive trade balance of $250 million, one of the two industries within the high technology sector to do so. The industry must continue to find new opportunities abroad to maintain the technological advances and ensure qualified human resources remain trained in the nuclear field. This will help maintain Canada's nuclear capability for future use when domestic demand for nuclear energy strengths. Future nuclear exports will help safeguard Canada's investment in the nuclear industry and will maintain nuclear as a viable energy option.

Notes

1. This contribution is based on estimates of the value of electricity generated from nuclear sources and the value of the Canadian content of exports of CANDU reactors. The first year that commercial volumes of electricity from nuclear sources were generated was 1962.

2. The employment data do not reflect the recent layoffs at Ontario Hydro. The total impacts of these layoffs are still unknown.

Document 5

The Nuclear Industry in Canada:
Ownership and Employment Trends
Restructuring and Adjustment in the Face of Declining Demand

Summary of a Report prepared by David Langille
for the Coalition of Environmental Groups
for a Sustainable Energy Future
January 1993

This report calls into question the perceived economic benefits of the nuclear power industry as a source of profits and jobs for Canadians. It features case studies of 27 firms in an effort to assess the degree of Canadian ownership and the employment conditions in the nuclear industry. Eighteen of these were manufacturing companies that had been studied by the management consulting firm Leonard & Partners, in a report they prepared for the Canadian Nuclear Association (CNA) in 1978. Nine other companies were added so as to offer a more representative sampling of the industry.

High Foreign Ownership

The nuclear industry continues to be dominated by foreign-owned companies. Of the 18 key firms that Leonard & Partners surveyed, 11 were foreign-owned in 1980, and 8 in 1992. Five have gone out of business or left the industry. Ninety percent of the companies listed in the *Nuclear Canada Yearbook 1981* were foreign-owned, while only 37 (8%) were Canadian-owned, and many of these were small engineering firms or consultants. In 1992, 61% of the suppliers listed were foreign-owned. Similarly, in 1992, 61% of the members of the Organization of CANDU Industries, which represents firms supplying goods and services for CANDU exports, were foreign corporations. This means that there were only 51 privately owned Canadian companies in the 1992 list of suppliers, i.e., 27% of the 189 firms. And there were only 12 Canadian companies belonging to the Organization of CANDU Industries, or 39% of the 31 members.

Foreign ownership matters a great deal in an era of free trade and global economic restructuring. Canadian governments end up subsidizing an outflow of investment capital rather than developing an indigenous industry. Instead of sustaining Canadian enterprises and Canadian employment, the benefits of government subsidies leak out of the country. This helps to explain why the industry cannot sustain itself or compete in international markets without ongoing infusions of public funds.

Many foreign-owned companies are rationalizing their operations due to the shortage of CANDU orders. Some, such as Babcock & Wilcox and the IST, have given their Canadian plants a mandate to export nuclear products; others such as Byron Jackson have closed their Canadian factories and shifted production to the US.

Fewer Firms Involved

Many companies have withdrawn from the nuclear industry because there has not been sufficient demand to justify the high costs of maintaining the necessary quality assurance standards, specialized machinery and skilled labour. The annual "Buyer's Guide" of nuclear products, materials and services published by the Canadian Nuclear Association listed 318 suppliers in 1976, 509 in 1981, 235 in 1990 and 189 in 1992. Among the firms that have chosen not to participate any further in the Canadian nuclear industry are Bristol Aerospace, Combustion Engineering, Dominion Bridge, Noranda, Titeflex, and Westinghouse. The decline of the nuclear industry has meant that others such as Guelph Engineering, Standard Modern, and Vickers Canada have gone out of business altogether.

Given the relatively high price of mining uranium in Ontario, both Denison Mines and Rio Algom have tried to diversify into other minerals and other countries before production at Elliot Lake ceases completely.

Declining Employment

Employment among the manufacturing firms surveyed declined by 53% between 1978 and 1992, from 38,161 to 17,987, a loss of 20,174 jobs. The number of persons working specifically on nuclear power dropped even more precipitously -- by 66%, from 3,469 to 1,169, a loss of 2,300 jobs. The loss of manufacturing jobs in the nuclear industry cannot merely be attributed to increased productivity, the current recession, economic restructuring, or free trade. During these years, overall manufacturing employment fell only by 8.2%, from 1,956,000 to 1,796,000.

Employment in the uranium mining and processing firms surveyed fell by 69% between 1980 and 1992, from 5,653 jobs to 1,755 jobs. This loss of 3,898 jobs has meant laying off over two-thirds of the workforce. Employment at AECL during the last ten years declined by 39%, as 2,824 jobs were cut, while Ontario Hydro hired 2,886 additional staff in this period, representing a gain of nearly 9%, and a 53% increase in its nuclear operations staff.

The overall decline in employment means that the nuclear power program is not a good vehicle for job creation. It offers relatively few ongoing jobs, and only at an enormous financial cost. There is also a high personal cost arising from such unstable employment, especially when the periodic slumps in demand threaten lay-offs on a month-by-month basis.

Trends and Prospects

Domestic and foreign markets are unable to sustain an ongoing, stable demand for CANDU goods and services. The current slowdown in the industry was well anticipated given that from 1980 on there was a 10 year gap in new orders. Although the orders for Wolsong will provide some work at a low level for the next five years, the industry will face a slowdown again in 1996 or 1997. The fault lies not with the Ontario Government's moratorium, but with the high cost and low performance of the existing reactors, and the downturn in demand leading to excess capacity. Meanwhile, the industry is counting on selling a CANDU 3 reactor to New Brunswick or Saskatchewan so as to demonstrate this new 'modular' technology to overseas customers. Many firms are also counting on the retubing and refurbishment of Ontario's reactors.

The collapse of uranium prices has meant the closing of the Elliot Lake mines, which was delayed until 1995 by the intervention of the Ontario government. Mining continues in Saskatchewan, where the ore is very rich and easy to mine, but uranium refining and processing have fallen off as world markets are flooded with low cost supplies.

Efforts to Maintain Industrial Capacity

While AECL and Ontario Hydro are concerned about sustaining their base of suppliers, their procurement policies do little to support Canadian-owned or 'home-base' enterprises. Although Hydro can offer Canadian suppliers a

10% price advantage, it very seldom does so. More effort has gone into the creation of the Nuclear Utilities Procurement Council, a clearinghouse for nuclear suppliers in Canada and the United States that will help create an integrated continental market for nuclear components. AECL and Ontario Hydro have also agreed to cooperate via the CANDU Engineering Business Plan, an effort to promote efficient utilization of resources and ensure "a viable CANDU product".

Prospects for Diversification, Conversion and Adjustment

The more diversified firms are better capable of surviving the downturn in nuclear business since they can shift to other lines of work, or from nuclear to thermal generating facilities. It is easier to shift to other work that requires the same skills, tooling and quality standards, such as aerospace and military production, but these sectors are also in decline. Such high quality assurance standards help to lower warranty claims, but may be too costly to maintain in the highly competitive marketplace for civilian goods. Conversely, firms that have concentrated more on nuclear business have suffered when there was a decline in reactor orders -- unless they produced a product for which there was a relatively steady demand.

Governments must investigate alternative employment possibilities for those employed in the nuclear industry, and alternative products and markets for the companies involved. Those suffering from the decline of the nuclear industry could produce equipment for non-utility generation or other energy efficiency strategies. The biggest stumbling block at the moment is Ontario Hydro's investment in nuclear power -- there is little demand for alternatives due to the surplus supply of nuclear-generated electricity.

Conclusions

The Canadian government's investment in the CANDU program has not proven viable as an industrial strategy. It has ended up subsidizing the profits of foreign corporations rather than developing an indigenous high technology industry capable of sustaining technological innovation and offering secure and stable employment. Continuing subsidies have been required in order to make the CANDUs 'competitive' in international markets.

Document 6

Selected information resources for further reference

Atomic Energy of Canada Ltd. (AECL)
344 Slater Street, Ottawa, Ontario K1A 0S4
Telephone (613) 237-3270, Facsimile (613) 782-2065

Canadian Energy Research Institute (CERI)
3512-33 Street NW, Calgary, Alberta T2L 2A6
Telephone (403) 282-1231, Facsimile (403) 284-4181

Canadian Nuclear Association
144 Front Street W., Ste. 725, Toronto, Ontario M5J 2L7
Telephone (416) 977-5211, Facsimile, (416) 979-8356

Canadian Renewable Fuels Association
90 Woodlawn Road W., Guelph, Ontario N1H 1B2
Telephone (519) 844-2191, Facsimile (519) 844-2741

Canadian Centre for Mineral and Energy Technology (CANMET)
555 Booth Street, Ottawa, Ontario K1A 0G1
Telephone (613) 995-4267, Facsimile (613) 995-3192

Energy Council of Canada
40 Colonnade Road, Ste. 400, Nepean, Ontario K2E 7J6
Telephone (613) 952-6469, Facsimile (613) 952-6470

Energy Probe
225 Brunswick Avenue, Toronto, Ontario M5S 2M6
Telephone (416) 964-9223, Facsimile (416) 964-8239

Friends of the Earth
251 Laurier Avenue W., F.7, Ottawa, Ontario K1P 5J6
Telephone (613) 230-3352, Facsimile (613) 232-4354

International Research Development Centre (IDRC)
250 Albert Street, PO Box 8500, Ottawa, Ontario K1G 3H9
Telephone (613) 236-6163, Facsimile (613) 563-0815

National Energy Board
311-6th Avenue SW, Calgary, Alberta T2P 3H2
Telephone (403) 292-4800

Nuclear Awareness Project
Box 2331, Oshawa, Ontario L1H 7V4
Telephone (905) 725-1565

Ontario Ministry of Environment and Energy
135 St. Clair Avenue W., Toronto, Ontario M4V 1P5
Telephone (416) 323-4321, 1-800-565-4923
Facsimile (416) 323-4564

Planetary Association for Clean Energy Inc.
100 Bronson Avenue, Ste. 1001, Ottawa, Ontario K1R 6G8
Telephone (613) 236-6265, Facsimile (613) 235-5876

Solar Energy Society of Canada Inc.
301 Moodie Drive, Ste. 420, Nepean, Ontario K2H 9C4
Telephone (613) 596-1067, Facsimile (613) 596-1120

Glossary

AECL	Atomic Energy Canada Ltd.
CAPP	Canadian Association of Petroleum Producers
CAPC	Canadian Auto Propane Council
CEMaC	Central Energy Management and Control
CERI	Canadian Energy Research Institute
CIDA	Canadian International Development Agencies
CIS	Commonwealth of Independent States
FSU	Former Soviet Union
FTA	Canada-US Free Trade Agreement
GATT	General Agreement on Tariffs and Trade
GDP	Gross Domestic Product
IAEA	International Atomic Energy Agency
IDRC	International Development Research Centre
IEA	International Energy Agency
MDIP	Market Development Incentive Payments
MITI	Ministry of International Trade and Industry (Japan)

MTBE	Methyl Tertiary Butyl Ether
NAFTA	North American Free Trade Agreement
NGV	Natural Gas for Vehicles
NRC	National Research Council
NUG	Non-Utility Generation
OECD	Organization of Economic Cooperation and Development
OEMs	Original Equipment Manufacturers
OPEC	Organization of Petroleum Exporting Countries
PWR	Pressurized Water Reactor
Tcf	Trillion cubic feet
TVA	Tennessee Valley Authority
UNCED	United Nations Conference on Environment and Development
UNEP	United Nations Environment Programme
VRAs	Vehicle Refuelling Appliances

The CISS gratefully acknowledges
the assistance provided by

AECL CANDU

ALBERTA ENERGY COMPANY LTD.

THE COOPERATIVE SECURITY
COMPETITION PROGRAM OF THE
DEPARTMENT OF EXTERNAL AFFAIRS
AND INTERNATIONAL TRADE CANADA

FOOTHILLS PIPE LINES LTD.

RANGER OIL LTD.

in support of the seminar

"Canadian Strategic Forecast 1994:
Preparing to Meet the Energy Challenges
of the 21st Century"

and the publication of these proceedings.